# GENEALOGY
## – for –
# BEGINNERS

## Arthur J. Willis
F.R.I.C.S., F.S.G.

and

## Karin Proudfoot
M.A.

## Phillimore

1997
Reprinted 1999


Published by
PHILLIMORE & CO. LTD.
Shopwyke Manor Barn, Chichester, West Sussex

ISBN 1 86077 041 X

Printed and bound in Great Britain by
REDWOOD BOOKS
Trowbridge, Wiltshire

# Contents

# List of Plates

# Abbreviations

| | |
|---|---|
| P.P.R. | Principal Probate Registry (Somerset House) |
| P.C.C. | Prerogative Court of Canterbury |
| P.C.Y. | Prerogative Court of Canterbury |
| P.R.O. | Public Record Office |
| B.L. | The British Library |
| Add. MSS. | Additional Manuscripts in the British Library |
| MS | Manuscript |
| I.G.I. | International Genealogical Index |

*Note:* Names and areas of counties are as existing before the 1974 reorganisation

*I cannot but condemn the carelessness, not to say ingratitude, of those ... who can give no better account of the place where their fathers and grand-fathers were born, than the child unborn ... I could almost wish that a moderate fine were imposed on such heirs, whose fathers were born before them, and yet they know not where they were born.*

Thomas Fuller, *The Worthies of England* (1662)

# Acknowledgements

M y thanks are due to those who have given permission for the reproduction of illustrations. The source is acknowledged at the foot of each plate.

I am also indebted to Anthony Camp, Director of the Society of Genealogists and to Carol Hartley for their help and suggestions. Lastly, I would like to thank my mother, Molly Tatchell, who so ably revised the last edition of this book – I hope I have lived up to her high standards.

Finally, apologies are due to my family, especially my husband, for dereliction of duty during the preparation of this book; their forbearance was much appreciated.

K.E.P.

# Preface

As modern life becomes ever more automated and impersonal, interest in the past increases, with a nationwide proliferation of 'heritage centres' and nostalgia galore on television and in print. The enthusiasm for discovering more about one's ancestors is a part of the heritage industry, and it shows no sign of abating. A quick glance round the bookshop at the Public Record Office, for example, will show countless guides to genealogy, both general and particular. Whether your ancestor was a Congregationalist or a Coastguard, there is a booklet to help you find out more.

The question facing a newcomer is, how to start? This book, whose first edition was published over forty years ago, aims to set the beginner on the right course, and for this latest edition, it has been extensively revised and, in parts, re-written to keep abreast of the latest developments.

In the 10 years since the last revision, we have had the release of the 1891 Census, an expansion in the wide availability of records on microfilm and microfiche, increasing use of computers by family historians (with whole books devoted to their needs) and, most recently, a major upheaval at the Public Record Office. The last documents have finally left the Victorian gothic splendour of Chancery Lane for the bleak functionalism of Kew, although pressure from various organisations has resulted in certain records being retained (on microfilm) for consultation in central London. Readers are, however, advised to check with the repository concerned before setting out as to the current whereabouts of particular records.

One of the most important developments has been the huge increase in the indexing of records – many census returns are now indexed, and the International Genealogical Index (a comparative novelty at the time of the last edition) is now a commonplace resource for searching parish registers, and is widely available.

As Arthur Willis says in his original Preface, this is a book for beginners, but the fully revised Bibliography will, I hope, point the way for those who progress beyond the scope of this book and need more specialised guidance.

I should also emphasise that I am dealing solely with research in England and Wales. Conditions and records are different in Scotland and Ireland, but the Bibliography includes guides to research in those countries.

K.E.P.

# Preface to the First Edition

An interest in genealogy need not be limited to those who are hoping to trace their descent from the Norman invaders, to revive a dormant peerage or, perhaps, just to gate-crash into 'County' society. There is much in the subject of interest for the ordinary man. We knew our fathers and probably our grandfathers. We may have heard tell of a great-grandfather. Who was he? What did he do? There is often little direct knowledge handed down, but, even if he had no exalted position, there is fairly certainly information about him somewhere – parish records, wills, local newspapers and similar sources. The records of his town or county may have lists of inhabitants, and these sometimes contain information as to place of business or residence. If he was a town councillor or interested in some local projects, charitable or otherwise, he may appear in the local archives. He may even be found in the records of the relief of the poor, or, perhaps, of the Quarter Sessions! A number of small details ca be collected which together may give some sort of picture.

Then what about his father? Information is naturally more difficult to find as one goes back, but, even if there is little detail about earlier generations, it may be quite possible, given a little luck, to trace the pedigree back to the 17th or even 16th century from parish registers, wills and other sources.

In making research into my own family pedigree I felt the need of an elementary guide on how to set about the undertaking, what to look for and where, the ordinary difficulties likely to be encountered and how they might be overcome. I was doing the research in spare time, so anything which would save me time in investigating methods of approach would be valuable. I could find nothing in the way of textbooks, except two or three small hand-books, which by trying to embrace too much gave little information of value to me. I have found in another sphere how much a textbook is appreciated on the very elements of a subject, untrammelled by the complications of more advanced work, and I thought that an elementary book, answering the queries and difficulties that I myself had met in my genealogical expedition, might be of value to others first taking up the subject, whether as a hobby or as a profession. I have, in Part I of the book, tried to meet this need.

May I emphasise that this is a book for beginners. The writing is focused on them and their needs: the expert cannot expect to find much, if anything, new. I am limiting myself to what might give the novice a start, and am excluding any consideration of the very early times (when both parish registers and regular records of wills are rare or non-existent) and of the remoter possibilities in later times. By the time any investigator has reached, say, the middle of the 16th century or has examined all the more normal sources of evidence in the later period he is more than a novice.

The plates are necessarily reduced in printing, but will be found to read clearly with the magnifying glass which should be in every genealogist's pocket.

In Part II I have given an account of the researches into my own family pedigree, and the relative tables necessary to follow it will be found on the chart (see pp.127-34). This account is but an example, an illustration of how a search can work out. If one is set a problem in geometry one does not expect to find all the standard theorems applied; some only will be needed. In the same way, this account does not hope to incorporate all the possible lines of research. It describes those which in a particular case were followed, some with success, some without. Some, such as the examination of parish registers, wills, etc., are essential to almost any search, some may or may not be suitable in other cases and one or two arose from the particular circumstances of the particular family and may never be applicable elsewhere. In other circumstances, moreover, there will be other methods of approach not touched on in the example. I hope that the account will convey something of the atmosphere of a search as well as provide suggestions as to methods and procedure. In preparing for an examination in geometry one will work out problems in past examination papers, not because the same will be set again, but because the course of reasoning may be useful in answering other questions.

I feel, too, that a real live example should be of value in showing that research need not be a dry-as-dust affair, but can be combined with light (and sometimes comic) relief in unveiling the lives of the individuals. I look on genealogy as something more than merely obtaining proof of descent: it is to me an attempt to answer the question 'Can these bones live?'

1955

A.J.W.

*James Willis* son of *Mary* John and *Mary Willis* born at Winchester 28th December 1834 married 7th May 1863 at the Parish Church of West Hackney, London. *Emma* eldest daughter of George and Jane Ashmwood, was born on the 20th day of June 1840 – Died 3rd Feby 1910 at Churchfield Rd. Ealing. Buried on 7th February by John, at the city of Westminster Cemetery Hanwell 13/2/10 Their children.

*James Herbert Willis* born at Gatley Road, Islington, London on the 4th of March 1864. Baptized at the Church of St Paul, Islington.

*Emma Lilian Willis* born at Southgate Road, Islington on the 12th of October 1865. Baptized at the Church of St Peter, De Beauvoir Square, London.

*Marian Ashmwood Willis* born at 116 De Beauvoir Road in the Parish of St Hackney, London, on the 3rd of May 1867. Died 12th of July 1868 and buried in the Cemetery Abney Park, London.

*Emma* wife of *James Willis* died on the 4th of May 1869 at No 116 De Beauvoir Road and was buried in the Cemetery at Abney Park on the 7th of May 1869, the 6th anniversary of her wedding day.

On the 14th of June 1873 the before mentioned *James Willis* married at the Parish Church of Cheriton near Sandgate, Kent, *Fanny Eleson Griffiths* daughter of George and Frances Griffiths of Long Buckby, Northamptonshire, who was born on the 19th of January 1851. Their children

A Son, stillborn on the 5th of September 1874.

*George Henry Willis*, born at 12 Eton Villas, Belgrave Road, Shepherds Bush, London, (now 41 Loftus Road) on the 21st of October 1875. Baptized on Christmas Day 1875 at the Parish Church of Norwood, Middlesex.

*John Burdett Willis*, born at 41 Loftus Road, Shepherds Bush on the 6th of March 1877.

The foregoing entries made by me, the before mentioned *James Willis* this 19th day of March 1877. *J Willis*

John Burdett Willis baptized at the Church of St Stephen Shepherds Bush on the 10th of June 1877 JW

**Plate 1** *An extract from a family Bible.*

CHAPTER 1

# How to Begin

When tracing a family tree, it is essential to start from the present and work backwards, one step at a time, establishing a firm descent for each generation before moving further back.

The tradition, or wishful thinking, of connection with some famous name one, two or more centuries ago should be put to one side until it is either confirmed by research, or, much more likely, shown to be erroneous. Otherwise one can fly off the track in many directions and be led into all sorts of by-ways and dead-ends, wasting both time and money.

The first step is to set down, in the form of a pedigree, what is already known of the family: your own name, those of your parents, uncles and aunts, grandparents, and so on, with dates and places where possible. This can be arranged as shown on the Willis pedigree at the end of the book (pp.127-34), with brothers and sisters in order of age from left to right, and wives next to their husbands.

This framework can then be filled out by asking older members of the family if they can add more detail. Opportunity should be taken to ask them to help by telling what they know, not just of the line of descent, but of the history of the family, their work, and the character of individual members whom they knew. It is at this point that the traditions of famous connections will make their appearance; these should be noted, but only as tradition, not definite knowledge, and put to one side for the time being.

Speaking of traditions, one of the most common is the connection with some armigerous family, supported by items bearing the 'family crest' which belonged to great-grandfather. It may, of course, be true, but it is wise to remain suspicious of such claims; in the 19th century, particularly, 'heraldic stationers' developed their publicity, and rings and notepaper with heraldic devices became common. Sadly, there is no such thing as a 'coat of arms for a surname'; each coat of arms should be used only by the male line descendants of an individual already on record at the College of Arms as being entitled to those arms. It follows that, in order to prove a right to arms, a pedigree must be submitted to the College, backed by appropriate evidences and entered in the official records. It was in innocent ignorance of these rules that our forebears aggrandised themselves by proudly displaying the arms and crest of another family of the same name.

Of much more use in tracing your family tree are records of names, dates and places, and you should ask about the existence of any old family papers which may include such information. There may well be a Family Bible, popular in the 18th and 19th centuries, and containing blank sheets for filling in important family events, such as births, marriages and deaths. A typical example of an extract from a family bible is given on plate 1 (see p.xvi). Even so, such entries may not include the names of places where the family was living at the time, and for this other sources are needed.

There may well be surviving copies of birth or marriage certificates, which will have valuable information, or even wills or records of burials or ownership of burial plots. Other documents that may be preserved include newspaper cuttings (maddeningly these have often been cut out and left undated!), letters, apprenticeship indentures, property deeds or leases, books (often given as Sunday School prizes and inscribed) and photographs. These last tend to be tucked away in old envelopes or boxes, and often the sitters are unidentified. It is well worth taking the time to show them to the oldest members of the family, in case they can name the people concerned, and any such information should immediately be written on the back, for the benefit of future generations. There is nothing more frustrating than coming across a potentially fascinating hoard of family photographs only to realise that there is no one still living who can identify them.

By now, you should have been able to add more details of dates and places to your outline pedigree and you will have exhausted the possibilities of research within your own family; the time has come for the first plunge into official records.

CHAPTER 2

# Records of Searches

**B**efore undertaking any genealogical research, it is essential that a careful record should be kept of all searches made, and the results, even if these are negative.

For taking notes an A4 notebook or pad could be used, and it is as well to be armed with a pencil, as many record offices do not permit the use of pen or ballpoint, for fear of marking or damage to the documents. The name of the library or record office should be noted at the top of the sheet, and each source marked with its reference, so that it can, if necessary, be looked up again in the future with the minimum of delay. If an index is being searched, or a number of years in a parish register, be sure to note down the years which have been covered, with any gaps if appropriate.

It will be found useful as soon as possible after taking notes to copy them in ink, or to type them, on to sheets of, say, A4 paper, each variety of record being on a separate sheet, so that their order can be rearranged. These sheets can then be kept in some sort of loose-leaf binder and, as they accumulate, they can be divided into several volumes, keeping some classification, such as one volume for parish registers, another for wills, and so on, subdividing them as necessary with index tabs. If two separate lines of descent are being traced (e.g. your father's and mother's ancestry) it will be found advisable to keep the records entirely separate.

Many amateur genealogists will want to make use of computers for recording the information they discover, and there are now many family history commercial and software packages available.

These are beyond the scope of this book, but a useful beginners' guide is produced by the Society of Genealogists: *Computers in Genealogy Beginners Hand Book*, which is available from the Society and is regularly updated (see p.63).

One should emphasise that it is just as important to keep a record of searches which produce no result as of those which do. I have more than once found myself looking at something which I had seen before, because I had not recorded that I had seen it. Much time can be wasted in that way.

It is worthwhile, too, recording all mention of the family name, even if there is no evidence of relationship at the time. Unexpected documentation may turn up later showing a connection, and it may be very difficult to remember where you saw the original reference.

On a purely practical note, it is well to get into the habit of always recording dates by separating the day of the month and the year, e.g. 2 December 1839, or even 1839 December 2. This prevents any confusion between the figures of the date and year. Where months are abbreviated, e.g. Jan., Jun., Jul., keep your writing quite clear to avoid subsequent mistakes.

Important or particularly interesting evidence may be photocopied. Most record offices are happy to provide this service, for a small charge, provided the document concerned is not in too fragile a condition, and, in the case of manuscripts which have been put on to microfilm, the process is easier still, as prints are made direct from the film. It can be useful to have photocopies of census returns, as any unclear names can be studied at leisure, with the help of a gazetteer in the case of place names. It is very satisfying to have a photocopy of a document which includes the signature of an ancestor, such as a will or a marriage licence bond and, especially in the case of wills, a clear copy can save a great deal of tedious copying of detail while at the record office.

Those interested in genealogy are normally in one of two categories: either the individual tracing his own family as a matter of personal interest and hobby, or somebody tracing ancestry for a specific purpose, such as a connection with an armigerous family, a matter of inheritance or other legal reason. In the first case proof has to satisfy only the searcher's conscience (which may vary in strictness with individuals), but in the latter it must satisfy the investigation of experts and have a legal standing. If serious proof is likely to be demanded, the original evidence of each step (or photoprint of it) should be kept with the pedigree so that it is there equally today or a hundred years hence.

It goes without saying that all new information will be transferred to the pedigree, which will, no doubt, need redrafting at intervals, as well as requiring the addition of extra sheets of paper, assuming that all goes well!

# CHAPTER 3

# Birth, Marriage and Death Certificates

B y now, you will probably have established a line of descent back to your grandparents or great-grandparents, or, with luck, even further back, but the information on the earlier generation or two is likely to be fairly sketchy, consisting of names, possibly places, and perhaps birthdays (though the actual year of birth may not be known).

The first port of call at this stage will almost invariably be the Family Records Centre, 1 Myddelton Street, London EC1R 1UW (off Rosebery Avenue), which, as from April 1997, now houses the records of all births, marriages and deaths in England and Wales since 1 July 1837 (6 and 7 Will. IV, c.85 and 86). From that date civil registration began, returns being sent to the General Register Office by District Registrars and, in the case of marriages in church, by the incumbent of the parish. Indexes may be searched without charge, the opening hours currently being 9.00 to 5.00, Monday, Wednesday and Friday, 10.00 to 7.00 on Tuesday, 9.00 to 7.00 on Thursday and 9.30 to 5.00 on Saturday. However, the information a genealogist requires will only be given in the form of a certificate; when the relevant entry has been found in the index, the details should be noted and a form filled in and handed in with the fee of £6. The certificate can then be posted (at no extra charge) or collected a few days later.

A word of warning is needed here: each year is divided into quarters (March, June, September and December), so to search one year involves looking in four separate volumes, each of which, at least for the earlier years, is large, very heavy and awkward to handle. It is as well to work out in advance exactly which years need to be searched, to avoid unnecessary effort. Remember, too, that a birth or death is listed under the date when it was registered, so that a birth on 27 March could well be indexed in the June quarter, if it were not registered until sometime in April.

The information given in the indexes is minimal, usually just the surname, Christian name(s) and registration district, so it is necessary to have some idea of the probable place and, if it is a village, the names of the nearest towns, which may well be the name of the registration district. If you are in difficulties, there are General Register Office guides listing the various registration districts, which can be consulted there.

If there is some doubt as to which of two or more entries in the index is the correct one, which can easily occur with a relatively common name, these entries can be checked against known details, at an additional charge, and only the correct certificate will be issued.

Incidentally, the Family Records Centre also includes registrations with British Consulates abroad, at which it is customary for British subjects to register births, marriages and deaths, and these are indexed in a separate series of volumes. One must not, therefore, necessarily be disheartened because an ancestor is found to have gone abroad.

If all this sounds too daunting, or it is not feasible to visit London, certificates can be applied for by post; the search fee for a period of five years is £15 including the cost of the certificate. It is important to provide as much information as you can in order that the correct entry can be identified, i.e. surname and Christian name, date and place of the event and, if possible, father's name.

Finally, a word about the sort of information that can be expected on a certificate; this can be summarised as followed:

| | |
|---|---|
| Births: | date and place of birth, full names of child, names of parents (including maiden name of mother), occupation of father and particulars of informant (usually mother or father) |
| Marriages: | date and place of marriage, full names and ages (sometimes whether of full age, i.e. over 21) of both parties, and whether bachelor, spinster or widowed, their occupations and addresses, full names and occupations of both fathers, the form of marriage and name of the person officiating, and the names of witnesses. |
| Deaths: | date and place of death, full name, sex, age and occupation of the deceased, cause of death and particulars of the informant. |

From this it can be seen that a line of descent can be traced back by means of a birth certificate, then the marriage of the parents, followed by the birth of the father, and so on, back to 1837. This is not only costly, but it also gives no information on brothers and sisters in each generation, nor on the environment in which the family was living. Certificates are best used in conjunction with census returns, which started (in their present form) at about the same time as civil registration, and are an invaluable source for genealogists.

For example, suppose that a birth has been found for 1863; a search of the census return for that place in 1861 would be the next step. If the family is found there, the place of birth of each member would be given (simplifying the search for the next birth certificate) and, with luck, a grandparent might be found living in the same household, or nearby. This could take one back another generation, and directly to the parish registers which are needed before the period of civil registration. If, however, the family is not found in the 1861 census, it is also worth trying that of 1871, or, perhaps, searching for the birth of an older child to give a clue as to the family's whereabouts in 1861.

CHAPTER 4

# Census Returns

A Census has been taken in England and Wales every 10 years from 1801 (except in 1941 during the Second World War). The earlier ones, which did not give names, have not, with one exception, survived, and those less than 100 years old are not yet open to inspection. But the Census Returns for 1841, 1851, 1861, 1871, 1881 and 1891 can be seen on microfilm at the Family Records Centre, 1 Myddelton Street, London EC1R 1UW, where they are now conveniently under the same roof as the records of births, marriages and deaths. The current opening hours are given in the previous Chapter (see page 7).

Of the above censuses, that for 1841 is the least useful. It gives the names, ages (within five years) and occupations of all persons in the household, but it does not give place of birth, beyond stating whether or not the individual was born in the county of residence.

The returns for 1851, 1861, 1871, 1881 and 1891 are more useful, for not only do they give the exact age (as alleged) and the relationship of the members of the household to one another, but, most important of all, they give the place of birth. In the case of a village or small town, it should then be easy to pin-point the parish register. Sometimes in the case of a large town or city, the parish of birth is given. If not, it can mean a search of a number of registers (not forgetting the non-Church of England ones). If place of birth is simply given as 'London', then one's heart truly sinks, as it can be a case of looking for the proverbial needle in a haystack.

For villages and small towns the first step is to look up the place name in a *Place Name Index* for the relevant census year,

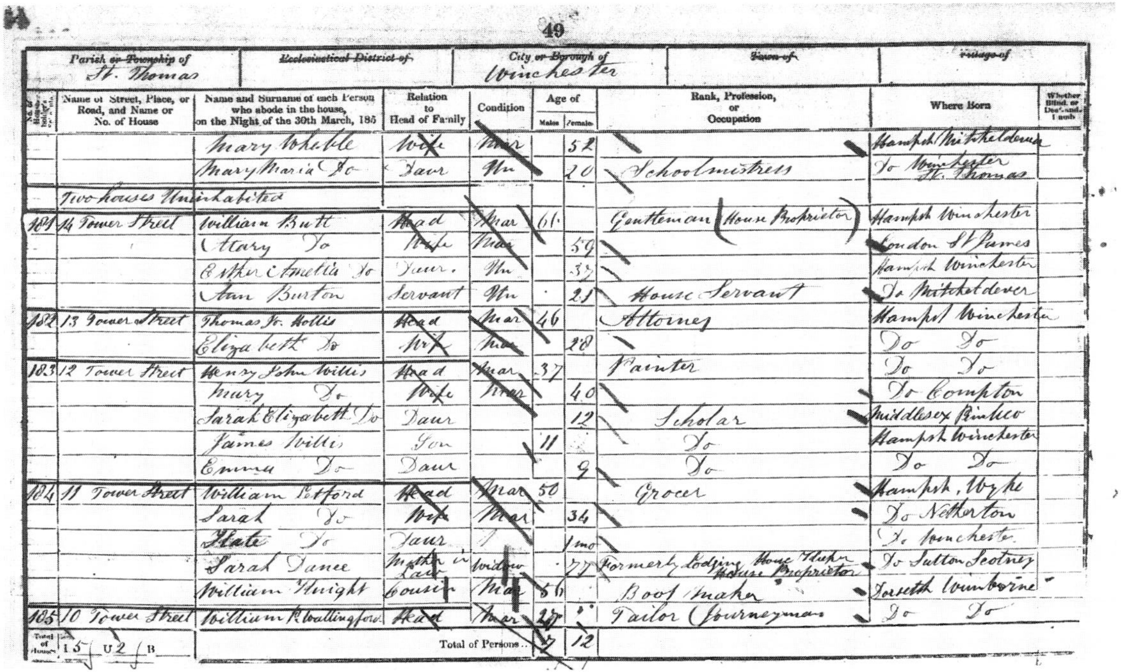

49

| Parish ~~or Township~~ of St. Thomas | ~~Ecclesiastical District of~~ | City ~~or Borough~~ of Winchester | ~~Town of~~ | ~~Village of~~ |
|---|---|---|---|---|

| No. of Householder's Schedule | Name of Street, Place, or Road, and Name or No. of House | Name and Surname of each Person who abode in the house, on the Night of the 30th March, 185 | Relation to Head of Family | Condition | Age of Males | Age of Females | Rank, Profession, or Occupation | Where Born | Whether Blind, or Deaf-and-Dumb |
|---|---|---|---|---|---|---|---|---|---|
| | | Mary Whebble | Wife | Mar | | 52 | | Hampsh Mitcheldever | |
| | | Mary Maria Do | Daur | Un | | 20 | Schoolmistress | Do Winchester St. Thomas | |
| | Two houses Uninhabited | | | | | | | | |
| 181 | 14 Tower Street | William Butt | Head | Mar | 61 | | Gentleman (House Proprietor) | Hampsh Winchester | |
| | | Mary Do | Wife | Mar | | 59 | | London St James | |
| | | Esther Amelia Do | Daur. | Un | | 37 | | Hampsh Winchester | |
| | | Ann Burton | Servant | Un | | 21 | House Servant | Do Mitcheldever | |
| 182 | 13 Tower Street | Thomas Jo. Hollis | Head | Mar | 46 | | Attorney | Hampsh Winchester | |
| | | Elizabeth Do | Wife | Mar | | 28 | | Do Do | |
| 183 | 12 Tower Street | Henry John Willis | Head | Mar | 37 | | Painter | Do Do | |
| | | Mary Do | Wife | Mar | | 40 | | Do Compton | |
| | | Sarah Elizabeth Do | Daur | | | 12 | Scholar | Middlesex Pimlico | |
| | | James Willis | Son | | 11 | | Do | Hampsh Winchester | |
| | | Emma Do | Daur | | | 9 | Do | Do Do | |
| 184 | 11 Tower Street | William Petford | Head | Mar | 50 | | Grocer | Hampsh, Wyke | |
| | | Sarah Do | Wife | Mar | | 34 | | Do Netherton | |
| | | Kate Do | Daur | | | 1 mo | | Do Winchester | |
| | | Sarah Dance | Mother in Law | Widow | | 77 | Formerly Lodging House Keeper House Proprietor | Do Sutton Scotney | |
| | | William Knight | Cousin | Mar | 56 | | Boot maker | Dorseth Wimborne | |
| 185 | 10 Tower Street | William R Wallingford | Head | Mar | 27 | | Tailor (Journeyman | Do Do | |
| Total of Houses | 15 U 2 B | | | Total of Persons | 7 | 12 | | | |

**Plate 2** *A census return (1851 Census of Winchester, Hampshire. P.R.O. Ref: Ho 107 1674). Crown Copyright. Reproduced by permission of the Controller of Her Majesty's Stationery Office.*

noting the yellow number which appears next to the place; then turn to a *Reference Book* and find the same yellow number there (in numerical order). From this note the 'class' code number in the lefthand column, and the 'piece' number below it which relates to the village to be searched. The 'class' codes are as follows: 1841 and 1851, HO 107; 1861, RG 9; 1871, RG 10; 1881, RG 11; 1891, RG 12.

For London and other large towns and cities exact addresses are essential in order to avoid an endless search. London directories for 1841-91 are available in the search room, but these only include tradesmen, professionals and people of substance.

There is a list, 'Table of Street Indexes' on the wall, which shows the availability of street indexes, and books in which streets can be looked up and the relevant class code and piece number found, as for smaller places.

There are also some name indexes compiled by various family history societies for the 1851 census, which are in cabinets in the census rooms, arranged by county or registration district. Some name indexes to the 1881 census are available, and are being added to as this project proceeds. A useful guide to these indexes is J. Gibson and E. Hampson, *Marriage, Census and other Indexes for Family Historians* (5th ed. 1994).

The census microfilms are in labelled cabinets, so once the correct reference has been found, the film can be taken out, replacing it with the dummy film which is by each reader.

One point to remember about census returns is that the information in them was supplied by the families themselves who may have had their own reasons for adjusting an age or place of birth, or may simply not have known the correct details. It is always worth trying to find the family in more than one census in case varying ages or places are given.

Many libraries and local record offices now hold microfilm copies of census returns which relate to their own area, and it is worth making enquiries about these before going to the Census

Room in London. Details of where copies may be seen are in *Census returns 1841-1891 on microfilm: a directory to local holdings* by J. Gibson (6th ed. 1994).

It is possible to obtain information from the 1901 census for a fee, but only the age and place of birth of a named person at an exact address will be supplied, and only to a direct descendant. Enquiries should be made at the Family Records Centre, where a form can be obtained.

A quick photocopying service is available, and copies are usually ready the same day, unless the counter is very busy, but copies can also be made using the reader printer, for which a token can be bought. In either case, the exact reference, including folio and page number, will be needed.

# CHAPTER 5

# Parish Registers

Until the order of Thomas Cromwell in 1538 there was no obligation to record baptisms, marriages and burials, though there are a few registers from an earlier date still extant. From that year the incumbent of the parish was required to keep such a record, but nevertheless a large number of the earliest registers have not survived. They were paper books at first until in 1597 it was ordered that they should be of parchment. Then they were apparently mostly transcribed, perhaps not without errors in so doing. Early volumes are in many cases missing, so one will face an advantage or handicap of good or bad luck in the search of a particular parish. It was also ordained in 1597 that copies of the register entries should be made and forwarded to the diocesan authorities. These copies are known as the 'Bishops' transcripts' and should be available to fill gaps where the original registers are lost, but, unfortunately, particularly in the earlier years, gaps will be found in these too.

During the Civil War, when what are known as Commonwealth 'intruders' took over parishes to the exclusion of the regular incumbents, the keeping of the registers became irregular. In 1653 under the Commonwealth the incumbent was often deprived of his authority over the registers, the keeping of which was transferred to a layman called a 'Register'. The solemnization of marriages was also soon after taken from the incumbent and the duty transferred to the justices. It will be found, therefore, that records of marriages during the Civil War and Commonwealth are often either missing or incomplete, though

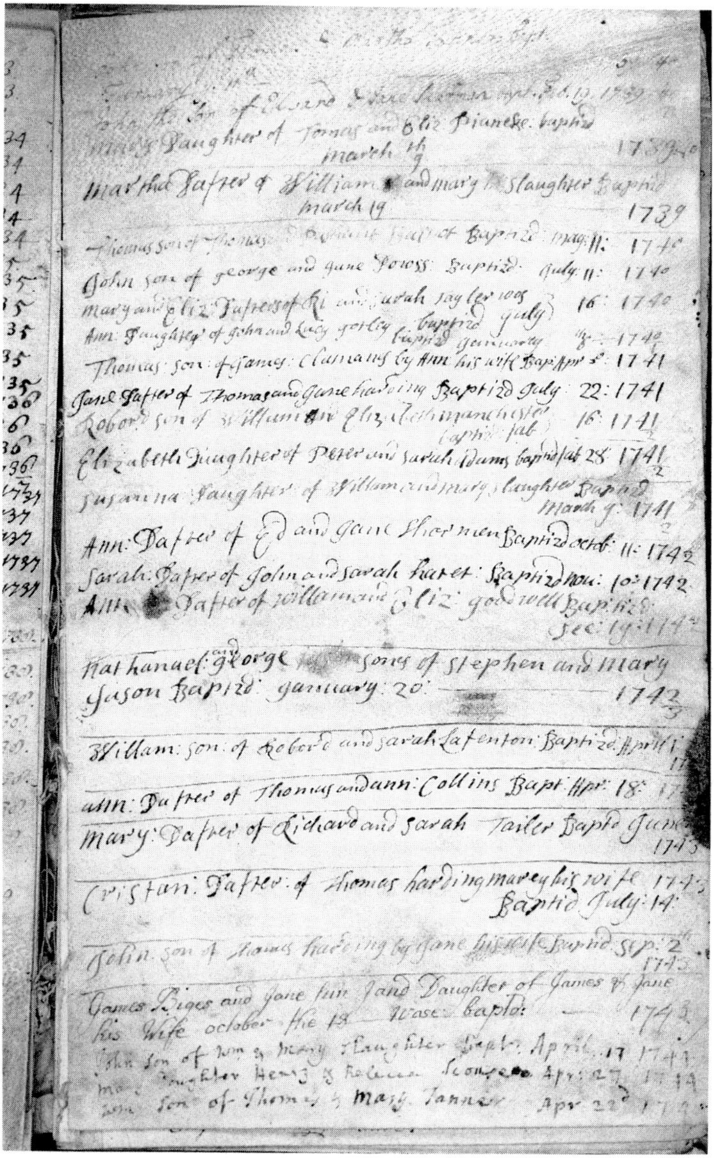

**Plate 3** *Entries from a Parish Register*
*(from the Parish Register, vol. 2, of Faccombe, Hants.).*
*(Reproduced by courtesy of the Hampshire Record Office.)*

fortunately the record of baptisms and burials may be found more regularly kept. The period and extent of the irregularity varies. In 1662 the intruders, if they did not 'conform', were often ejected. In 1754, following Lord Hardwicke's Marriage Act (26 Geo II, c.33) record was to be kept of banns as well as marriages and the register was to be signed by the parties. Books of printed forms became available for this. They are not always to be found, but should be looked for.

Under Rose's Act of 1812 (52 Geo. III, c.146) the registers were to be kept in three separate volumes in official printed form, and in smaller parishes where there are few entries the baptisms and burial volumes will be found still in use to this day.

On 1 July 1837 the system of civil registration now in force began, as has already been mentioned (p.7). Baptism and burial (as distinct from birth and death) records were continued in the churches. Marriages, instead of being included in the bishops' transcripts, were returned in the standard form to the Registrar General, though they are found to a limited extent in the transcript.

Parish registers are, therefore, the main source of information for family history prior to 1837, and once a family line has been traced back as far as possible through birth, marriage and death certificates, and census returns, the next stage is to search for the baptism of the earliest known ancestor. The place and approximate year of birth will have been established from census returns, and the registers of the appropriate parish need to be located and examined.

It is worth remembering that large towns and cities include several different parishes, each with its own registers, and also that the place of birth given in a census may not itself be a parish, but could be a hamlet in a parish of another name.

An invaluable guide for identifying parishes and locating their registers is *The Phillimore Atlas and Index of Parish Registers* (1995), which includes pre-1837 topographical maps and modern maps showing parish boundaries and probate jurisdictions, with comprehensive lists of all parishes, arranged by county, giving details of which registers survive, and where, and also the availability of copies and indexes. Some counties are also covered by *The National Index of Parish Registers* (Society of Genealogists, 1968-), a continuing project.

Before consulting the actual registers, it is worth investigating one or more of the centralised indexes which cover some, though not all, parish registers. These can be particularly useful if a place of birth is uncertain.

The most important of these is the International Genealogical Index, which has been widely available for many years, and can be consulted at the Society of Genealogists and the Guildhall Library in London, county record offices, Mormon Family History Centres and many large libraries.

It was originally conceived as an index, on microfiche, to the filmed copies of parish registers made by the Church of Latter Day Saints (the Mormons) and stored in Utah. However, its potential value to genealogists persuaded the Mormon authorities to allow copies to be made for other libraries, the first being sent to the Society of Genealogists. The latest (1992) edition contains more than 187,000,000 names from around the world.

The microfiches for this country consist of an alphabetical index, arranged by county, of births, baptisms and marriages, but before seizing on it as the answer to every genealogist's prayer a few words of warning are needed. Firstly, it does not offer comprehensive coverage of every parish in the country, nor does it include deaths and burials; *The Phillimore Atlas and Index of Parish Registers* lists those parishes and years which are included. Furthermore, the entries are not only in a standardised form, but variant spellings of surnames and Christian names can be indexed in a most illogical way, often separately from their most usual form, so care is needed to check all possible variations, however improbable. Finally, do bear in mind that this is an Index, and was only intended as such, so any possibly relevant entries should be checked against the original sources, usually parish registers; inevitably mistakes have crept in, due to human error and poor legibility of the original.

Within its limitations, however, the I.G.I. can be a godsend, especially in cases where a family moved around a lot, when a wide geographical area can be scanned in a short time. It can also be useful in tracking down other members of a family in a particular parish, especially a large one, where to search the registers year by year would be tedious and time-consuming task. In short, use it as an aid but not a primary source.

A useful guide to the complexities of the I.G.I. is *Making the Most of the I.G.I.* by Eve McLaughlin (1992 and subsequent revisions).

Marriages from many counties are indexed in Boyd's Marriage Index, at the Society of Genealogists, which is more fully described in Chapter 10 (see p.65). This gives only the barest information: surname and Christian name of the bride and groom, and the year and parish of the marriage, so more detail must be sought from the parish register concerned.

Marriages in the London area only are included in Pallot's Marriage Index, which covers most entries in the years 1780-1837. There are no copies of this index, and applications for searches should be made by post to Achievements Ltd., 79-82 Northgate, Canterbury, Kent CT1 1BA; a minimum fee of £12 is payable. However, for this often difficult period in London immediately before civil registration this index can provide just the clue that is needed.

Other county indexes are being compiled by local family history societies and by individuals, who will undertake searches for a small fee. Details can be found in *Marriage, Census and other Indexes for Family Historians* by J. Gibson and E. Hampson (Federation of Family History Societies, 5th ed. 1994).

As already mentioned, all entries from indexes should be checked in the original registers, or, if this is not possible, in a good copy. The Society of Genealogists has the largest collection of parish register copies in the country, listed in *Parish Register Copies in the Library of the Society of Genealogists* (11th ed. 1995), and there are many printed copies available in local record offices and libraries.

Virtually all original parish registers are now held in county record offices and a few other libraries, and these can generally be visited free. In the rare instances where the registers are still in the parish, an appointment should be made with the incumbent (enclosing a stamped addressed envelope for reply), who is entitled to charge a fee, currently £11 for the first hour and £9 for each subsequent hour or part of an hour.

In view of the greatly increased number of people wishing to consult registers (and other documents) and record offices, it is advisable to telephone in advance to check on the availability of the required records and, if necessary, to book a seat, particularly if the registers concerned are on microfilm, in which case a microfilm reader may need to be booked.

Unless the beginner has prepared himself, he may be disappointed when he first sees a parish register, because he finds he cannot read the earlier entries. The hands of the 16th and 17th centuries and even the 18th are difficult to decipher until one is accustomed to them. Photocopies of wills or other documents could be obtained and studied at leisure instead of at a repository which may be distant from home. A book such as *Reading Tudor and Stuart Handwriting* or *Examples of English Handwriting 1150-1750* (see Bibliography, p.86) will be found useful. The latter reproduces documents photographically and includes a printed transcript of each. Similar help may be found from the will and inventory on plates 5 and 6 of this book and their transcripts on facing pages. It will be found that by comparing letters of unknown words with those of words which are obvious, the alphabet in use can gradually be built up. Although, perhaps, more care was taken in writing in the past, there was good and bad writing then just as there is today, and, even when some knowledge of the letters used has been acquired, it may take time to become accustomed to individual handwriting. The genealogist should always carry a pocket magnifying glass to help him to decipher letters which are difficult, covered by blots or faint from age.

The arrangement of a parish register will not always be found orderly. Baptisms and burials may be intermixed and in the earlier days marriages too may be found in the same sequence. Sometimes facing pages will be used as a means of separation, sometimes opposite ends of the volume (so don't forget to look at the back end!). Volumes do not usually end completely at a fixed date. If the pages allotted to baptisms are filled, the incumbent may have started a new book for them but continued the entry of marriages and burials in the old book.

Even when separation is attempted, a stray item may be in the wrong place. In examining the registers of a parish from which the marriages had been printed, I found a marriage in among the burials which had not been found by the editor of the printed volume. A series of pages which appears to be blank should be carefully examined. It may be that two or three pages in the middle have been used.

One must remember, too, that the registers were sometimes kept on loose sheets which were bound up afterwards, when the sheets may have been sewn up in the wrong order. If there is no date at the top of the page, this may be very confusing. Pages should be checked to see that they are in proper serial order.

It was not uncommon for the incumbent to go round to private houses for baptisms, sometimes to baptise several infants in one house. He made his records on slips of paper, which may not have been copied into the register – such slips have been found at the bottom of the parish chest. Entries in the register, moreover, were often made weekly, and it was not difficult to forget to make one, as anybody knows who tries to make up his diary two or three days late. Sometimes the parish clerk kept the entries in a notebook, and entries have been found in such a book which are not in the official register.

Parish registers are not necessarily conclusive evidence that an infant grew up to be an adult, as burials are sometimes missing. This may, perhaps, explain some of the cases of unusual longevity. A son John is baptised, say in 1700, and dies in the same year, the burial record being omitted. Ten or even 20 years later another son is baptised with the same name (quite common, and in early days not unusual even when the first was still alive) and survives. His burial appearing in, say, 1780, may be related to the first baptism in error. It may be that only a will, naming sons in order of seniority, brings the error to light.

It must not be forgotten that quite often the first child was baptised (and even buried when dying in infancy) in the mother's parish. A bride dying young may also be found buried in the parish of her childhood.

In the parish register will sometimes be found more than the bare records of names. The parish of a stranger, a description such as 'widow', a man's trade, given perhaps to distinguish two of the same name, all provide valuable evidence. A list of pew-holders is quite common and may sometimes be useful as evidence that a particular man was still in the parish at its date. A record of 'briefs' sometimes found may serve a similar purpose. These 'briefs' were a royal direction for contributions to some specific worthy object and have been described as 'almost an early equivalent of the Mansion House Fund or "this week's good cause" ' (*The Parish Chest*, Tate). The contributions received were sometimes entered in full detail in the registers. A variety of other records and notes will be found, mostly of historical rather than genealogical interest.

Spelling will be found to be very erratic in the registers. Entries were often made by the parish clerk who spelt more or less phonetically: perhaps, too, he was sometimes a little deaf! One must remember that education (if reading and writing may be called education) is a product of a later age, and that in the 17th and 18th centuries there were comparatively few in a village who could read and write. On reference to the register entries on plate 3 (see p.15), such words as Willam, Robord, Marey will be seen. If there are such mistakes in spelling with common Christian names, it is not surprising that surnames get distorted. For instance, 'Lafenton' on that page should, judging from baptism records elsewhere in the register, probably be 'Lavington'. It was, however, not ignorance only that was responsible; spelling, up to about the end of the 18th century, just did not matter. All varieties of a surname must therefore be taken together, though they should in each case be copied in the exact spelling found. In my own case I have come across Willis, Willes, Wyllys, Willys, Wilis, Willowes, Willice or Wilce, all obviously referring to the same name. It is quite possible that sometimes the name has been written as Wills, but I have only followed up that name where there should be a likelihood of connection.

In reading parish registers one must remember the method of dating before the present-day calendar came into force in 1752. There used to be two methods of dating: one, that of the Church and the legal world, began the year at the Feast of Annunciation (i.e. Lady Day, 25 March), the other, used for historical purposes, beginning on 1 January. Consequently, an entry in a parish register of say, 3 February 1723, would be February in historical year 1724, and in pedigrees and other present-day references should be described as 3 February 1723/4. As from 1 January 1752, the year began for all purposes on 1 January (24 Geo. II, c.23). Reference to an extract from a register reproduced on plate 3 (see p.15) will show where the changes in the year came. For instance, consecutive entries are dated December 1742 and January 1742/3.

Parish registers are probably the most important source of genealogical information and the first to be examined after the Birth, Marriage and Death Records and Census Returns have been disposed of. Sometimes, however, they are not conclusive by themselves. Confusion may arise where fathers of the same

Christian name and surname had children baptised in the same parish and over a similar period. Baptisms in later years usually give the name of father and mother, so a 'John, son of John and Alice X' will be known to be of a different family from 'Peter, son of John and Mary X'. If, however, the mother's name is not given in the register, as is often the case with early entries, and they merely appear as 'John, son of John X' and 'Peter, son of John X' there is nothing to separate the families. Here comes the value of wills, though, as will be seen in Chapter 7, the making of wills was not so common in the past as it is today.

A grandfather's will may refer to his son John and his children Peter, James and Henry, whereas another may refer to son John and his children, John, George and Alice. Baptisms of all will quite possibly have appeared in the same register but the wills sort out the families. The will, of course, need not necessarily be the grandfather's; it might be that of any relation.

Where registers are missing or gaps appear, enquiry should be made as to the existence of the Bishops' Transcripts referred to above. Although the Bishops' Transcripts are archives of the Diocesan Registry, in most dioceses they will be found deposited elsewhere. They may be at the County Record Office; if not, the County Archivist will be able to confirm where they are. The transcripts may be in bundles by years rather than arranged by parishes; if so, a good deal of time may be needed to search one particular parish over a number of years. Particulars and location of these transcripts are given in the *National Index of Parish Registers* (mentioned above, p.17). Another useful guide is J. Gibson's *Bishops' Transcripts and Marriage Licences, Bonds and Allegations* (3rd ed. 1991), which covers the whole country, including counties not yet in the *National Index*; it gives the location and starting dates of the transcripts, which varies from one diocese to another.

In some dioceses there may be detailed lists, such as the *Handlist of Leicestershire Parish Register Transcripts* (City of Leicestershire Department of Archives). Transcripts of some registers of consular offices and Anglican chaplaincies abroad were sent to the London diocese and are now in Guildhall Library, London, who publish a list.

Even if the parish registers have been seen, it is as well to see the bishops' transcript, if available, when some expected entry cannot be found. Entries have been discovered in the transcripts which do not appear in the registers, which seems to indicate that the parson sometimes kept a rough list or book and did not enter up the register till after he had sent in the transcript.

The parish registers are, of course, those of the established Church of England. Though Nonconformists (or Dissenters) were not regular members of the established Church, they still, in their earlier days at any rate, were often baptised, married or buried there; indeed, following Lord Hardwicke's Marriage Act of 1754 everyone except Quakers and Jews had to be married in an Anglican church, a law which remained in force until 1837.

At the beginning of civil registration in 1837 nonconformist bodies were asked to send their registers to the Registrar General, and these are now available on microfilm at the Family Records Centre (see page 7). A list of them has been published (*List of Non-Parochial Registers in the Custody of the Registrar General*, H.M.S.O. 1859) and may be seen there, or will be found in some of the principal libraries. It will be seen that, generally speaking, the Roman Catholic and Jewish denominations did not do this, and their records must be looked for elsewhere. Moreover, there was no doubt neglect by others of the request, so that there is no guarantee that there are none extant in other places.

The Catholic Record Society has published certain Roman Catholic registers and the Huguenot Society of London some of those of French Protestants in this country. Some useful articles have been written on both the Huguenot and Jewish problem.* If no record can be found from any of the above sources, inquiry should be made from the present authority of the denomination in the locality concerned as to whether any old records survive in their custody. The Society of Friends (Quakers) have their own central repository of records at Friends' House, Euston Road, London NW1 2BJ, which should be visited by anybody following ancestors of that persuasion. Though their registers should be with the non-parochial registers at the P.R.O., the Society made copies before surrendering them.

When the possibilities of parish registers have been exhausted, the most valuable source of information will be the record of wills and administrations. But, while the opportunity is there, examination should be made of other parish documents which will be found kept with the registers or otherwise in the charge of the incumbent. Something will be said of the value of these in the next chapter before dealing with the subject of wills.

* *Huguenot Ancestry*, N. Currer Briggs & R. Gambier (1985). The *My Ancestors were* ... series of guides (Society of Genealogists) includes booklets on Methodist, Baptist, Congregationalist and English Presbyterian/Unitarian ancestry, as well as Jews and Quakers.

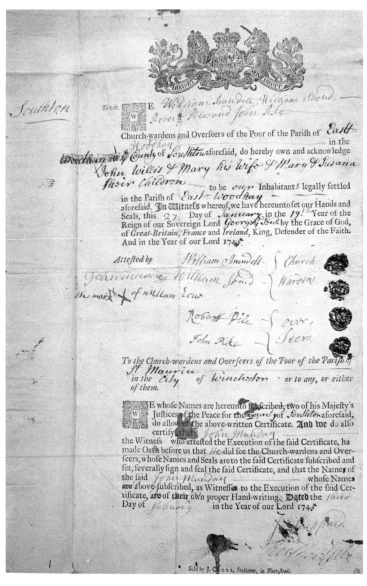

**Plate 4**   *A Settlement Certificate (from the Parish Records of St Maurice, Winchester).*
*(Reproduced by courtesy of the Hampshire Record Office.)*

# CHAPTER 6

# Other Parish Records

The majority of surviving parish records, other than the registers, are either concerned with the administration of Church funds or with the responsibility of the parish to the poor.

The general expense accounts of churchwardens are not likely to help much with the proof of a pedigree, but they often mention names of those to whom payment is made, and some information may be gathered of their status accordingly.

The records of rates levied are more useful. From quite early times the parishioners assembled as a 'vestry' had the power to levy a church rate for maintenance of the church fabric or other such purpose: later they were also responsible for making a rate to support the poor. The rate book of the parish, where surviving, will be found to record the names of parishioners and their assessments, so providing, like the lists of seatholders sometimes found in the registers, useful evidence of who was in the parish at the time and giving some idea of their substance. An example will be seen in a later chapter of a valuable genealogical clue given by rate books (see p.120).

However, perhaps the most valuable parish records for the genealogist, after the registers, are the 'settlement certificates' (see plate 4), sometimes found amongst parish papers, because by them can be proved the removal of a family, often otherwise very difficult to trace. These certificates were a result of the increasing burden of the poor on a parish. An Act of 1601 (43 Eliz. I, c.2) laid down that overseers were to be appointed to act with the churchwardens in maintaining the poor and providing them with work, and in

1662 another Act (14 Car. II, c.12) gave authority for removal of a stranger to his own parish unless he rented a property of the value of £10. It was by an Act of 1697 (8 and 9 W. and M., c.30) that the system of settlement certificates was established. A poor man was very restricted in his movements and was liable to be sent back to his own parish to be maintained there, if the necessity arose. He could acquire a settlement in a new parish under certain conditions, but, if he looked like being a charge on the parish, the authorities naturally did all they could to prevent a settlement. They had power to require him to obtain from his own parish a certificate that he was settled there, such certificate giving an undertaking to receive him back. These certificates were carefully kept as the authority for returning a man, and by that chance it has become sometimes easier to trace the movements of a poor family than those of the more prosperous classes. With the certificates may sometimes be found records of the declaration of their circumstances which these men had to make and such records often give information of family descent (see *Winchester Settlement Papers 1667-1842*, Arthur J. Willis, 1967). Removal orders arising from the settlement certificates are also sometimes found.

Since the churchwardens and overseers were responsible for putting the poor to work they were often parties to apprenticeship deeds. They were empowered to place apprentices with the consent of the justices, and indentures may be found with the parish documents, again throwing light on the movement of the poorer members of the community. In some cases a borough would undertake the placing of apprentice (see *A Calendar of Southampton Apprenticeship Registers, 1609-1740*, Arthur J. Willis and A.L. Merson, Southampton Records Series, 1968).

Records of marriage licences (see p.45) may sometimes be found, particularly where the incumbent was a surrogate for granting licences. Their value is obvious.

Tithe maps are parish records but copies are now in the Public Record Office and in the various county record offices. For further details see p.79.

A great variety of other documents may be found from incumbents' diaries to certificates for touching for the King's evil (i.e., a certificate from the minister and churchwardens that a sufferer from scrofula had not before received the Royal touch which was supposed to cure it). When the parish of the family whose genealogy is being traced has been ascertained, all documents in the parish chest or vestry cupboard should be examined for possible evidence. This may mean spending a long time, as there are not likely to be indexes, but it is a 'must'. In many cases all such documents may have been transferred to the County Record Office, so enquiry should be made there first.

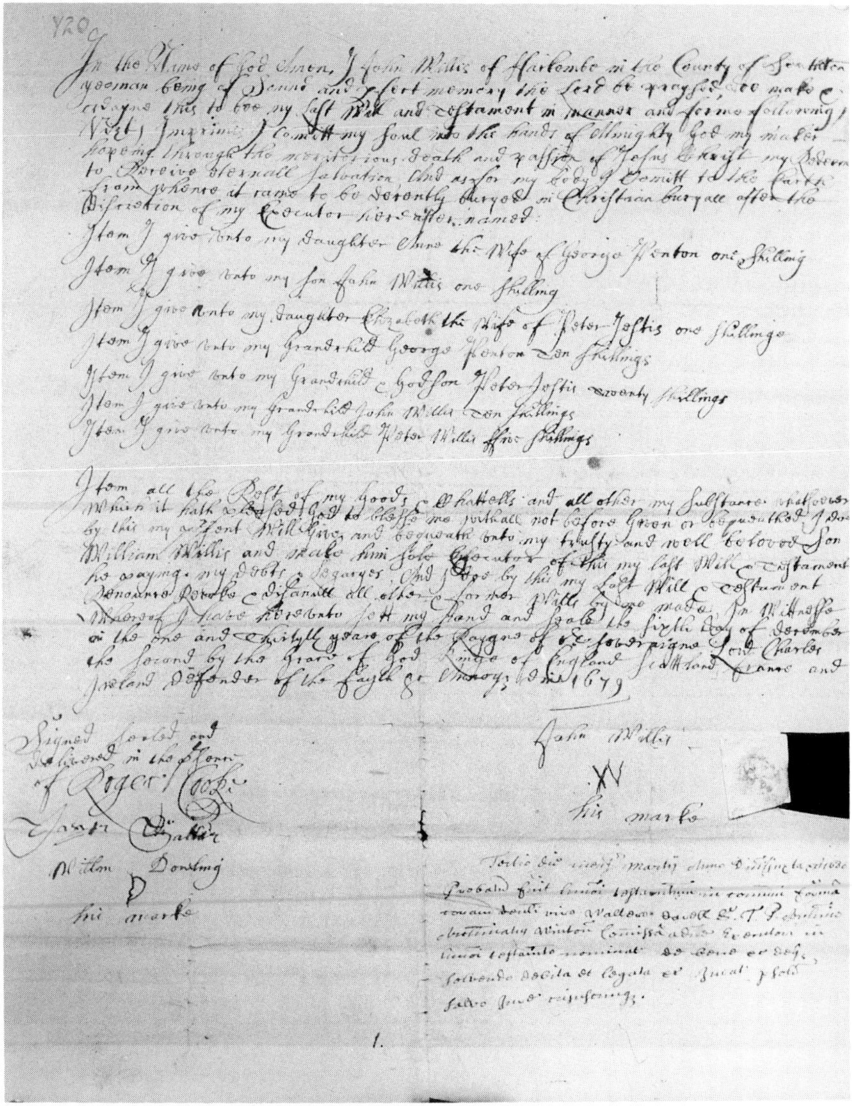

**Plate 5** *A 17th-century Will (from the District Probate Registry, Winchester, Archdeacon's Court 1860). (Reproduced by courtesy of the Hampshire Record Office.)*

# TRANSCRIPT OF PLATE 5

In the Name of God Amen, I John Willis of Fackombe in the County of Southampton, yeoman, being of sound and perfect memory the Lord be praysed, doe make and ordayne this to be my last Will and Testament in manner and forme following vizt.: Imprimis I committ my soul into the hands of Almightly God my maker hopeing through the meritorious death and passion of Jesus Christ my Redeemer to receive eternal Salvation. And as for my body I committ to the Earth from whence it came to be decently buryed in Christian buryall after the discretion of my Executor hereafter named

Item I give unto my daughter Anne the wife of George Penton one shilling
Item I give unto my son John Willis one shilling
Item I give unto my daughter Elizabeth the wife of Peter Jestis one shillinge
Item I give unto my grandchild George Penton ten shillings
Item I give unto my grandchild and godson Peter Jestis twenty shillings
Item I give unto my grandchild John Willis ten shillings
Item I give unto my grandchild Peter Willis five shillings
Item all the rest of my goods and chattels and all other my substance whatsoever which it hath pleased God to blesse me withall not before given or bequeathed I doe by this my present Will give and bequeath unto my trusty and well beloved son William Willis and make him sole executor of this my last Will and Testament he paying my debts and legacies. And I do by this my last Will and Testament renounce revoke and disannull all other and former wills by me made. In Witnesse whereof I have hereunto sett my hand and seale the sixth day of December in the one and thiryeth yeare of the raygne of the Sovereign Lord Charles the Second by the Grace of God Kinge of England Scottland france and Ireland defender of the fayth etc. annoque domini. 1679

Signed sealed and
delivered in the
psence of

Roger Cooke
Jasper Salter
William, Dowling
D
his marke

John Willis
W
his marke

tertio die mens. Martii anno Dni (juxta &c.*) 1680 probatum fuit hmoi. (hujusmodi) testamentum in communi forma coram venli. (venerabili) viro Waltero Darrell S.T.P. (Sacrae Theologiae Professori) Archino (Archidiacono) Archinatus Winton. Commissa adm(inistratio) executori in hmoi. testamento nominat(o) de bene etc. denique solvendo debita et legata etc. Jurato personaliter salvo Jure cuiuscunque.†

* Elsewhere found to represent 'juxta cursum et computacionem Ecclesie Anglicane'.

† On the third day of the month of March in the year of Our Lord 1680/1 the said will was proved in common form in the presence of the Venerable Walter Darell, D.D., Archdeacon of Winchester. Administration was granted to the executor named in the said will, he having personally sworn to administer justly and pay the debts and legacies etc. without prejudice to the rights of any other person.

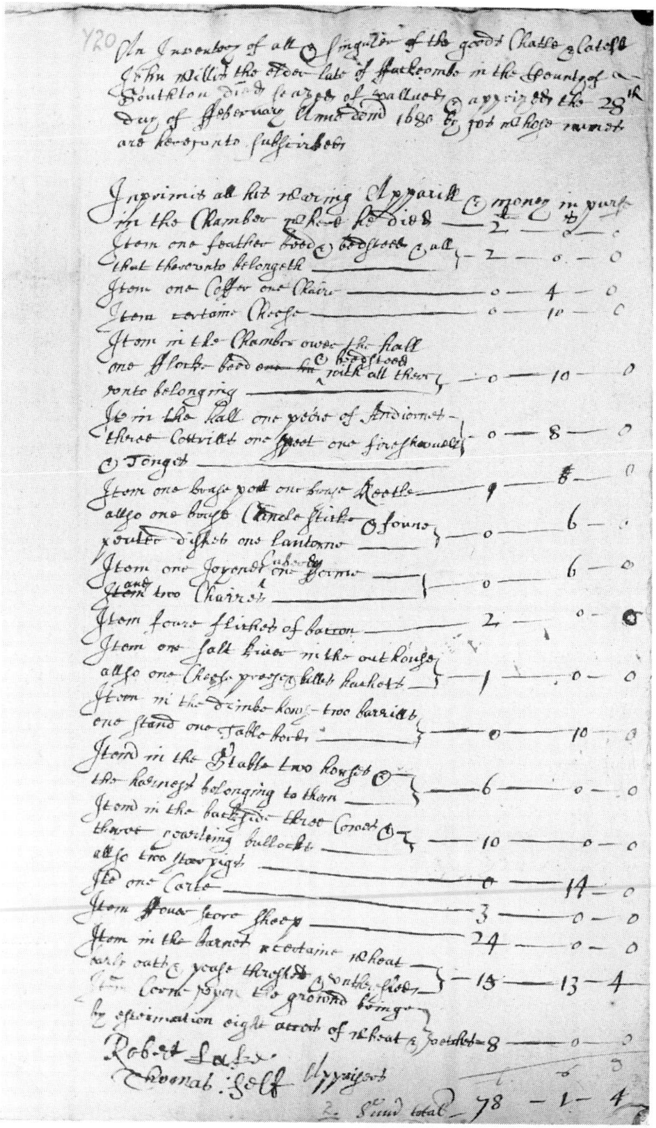

**Plate 6** *An Inventory found with the Will on Plate 5 (from the District Probate Registry, Winchester). (Reproduced by courtesy of the Hampshire Record Office.)*

# Transcript of Plate 6

An inventory of all and singular the goods chatle and catell late of John Willis the elder late of Fackoombe in the County of Southampton died seazed of valued and apprized the 28th day of February anno domi 1680 by us whose names are hereunto subscribed.

| | li | s | d |
|---|---|---|---|
| Imprimis all his wearing apparill and money in purse in the chamber where he died | 2 | 0 | 0 |
| Item one feather beed & bedsteed & all that thereunto belongeth | 2 | 0 | 0 |
| Item one coffer one chaire | | 4 | 0 |
| Item certaine cheese | | 10 | 0 |
| Item in the chamber over the hall one Flocke beed & bedstead with all thereunto belonging | | 10 | 0 |
| Item in the hall one peere [pair] of andiornes [andirons] three cottrils one speet one fireshoovell & tonges | | 8 | 0 |
| Item one brase pott one brase keetle allso | 1 | 0 | 0 |
| one brase candlesticke & foure peuter dishes one lanterns | | 6 | 0 |
| Item one joyend cubord one Forme and two chaires | | 6 | 0 |
| Item foure fliches of baccon | 2 | 0 | 0 |
| Item one salt kiver in the outhouse allso one cheese preese and billet hatchets | 1 | 0 | 0 |
| Item in the drinke house two barrils one stand one table bord | | 10 | 0 |
| Item in the stable two horses and the harness belonging to them | 6 | 0 | 0 |
| Item in the backside two cowes and three yearling bullocks | 10 | 0 | 0 |
| allso two store pigs | | 14 | 0 |
| Item one carte | 3 | 0 | 0 |
| Item Fouer score sheep | 24 | 0 | 0 |
| Item in the barnes certaine wheat barly oats & pease threshed and unthreshed | 15 | 13 | 4 |
| Item come upon the ground being by estimation eight acres of wheat & vetches | 8 | 0 | 0 |
| Sum total | 78 | 1 | 4 |

(sgd) Robert Lake

Thomas Self — Appreisers

CHAPTER 7

# Wills and Administrations

Before 1858 wills were a matter for ecclesiastical authority. Early wills will be found nearly always opening with a prayer for the testator's soul, committal of his body to the churchyard of his parish, sometimes followed by a legacy to the Church, before attention is turned to secular matters. The will was proved in the Court of the archdeacon or bishop within whose archdeaconry or diocese respectively the property was held, except where some incumbent or other authority had 'peculiar' jurisdiction excluding these Courts. Where property was held in more than one archdeaconry of a diocese the will had to be proved in the bishop's Court, if in more than one diocese in the Prerogative Court of the Province – i.e., Canterbury or York. The exact rules deciding which was the proper Court in which to prove a will are now rather obscure, as there were periods during a 'visitation' when one minor Court was 'inhibited' and recourse must be had to a superior authority. The above general rule will, however, give a guide as to where to look first. If a particular will is not found where it may be expected, the possibility of a Superior court should be examined. During the Commonwealth from about 1652 to 1660 ecclesiastical jurisdiction in the matter of wills was suspended and all wills had to be proved before a civil authority in London. These wills are now at the P.R.O. On the restoration jurisdiction was restored to the Church.

By the Court of Probate Act of 1857 (20 & 21 Vic., c.77) the Principal Probate Registry was established in London with a number of District Registries subordinated to it, and the Church was finally deprived of the jurisdiction. The wills and other records of the ecclesiastical probate courts were handed over to other authorities, and are now in the care of local County Record Offices or Libraries. The records of the Prerogative Court of Canterbury (including wills proved during the Commonwealth period, as mentioned above) are at the P.R.O. Those of the Prerogative Court of York are at the Borthwick Institute of Historical Research, St Anthony's Hall, Peaseholme Green, York YO1 2PW.

In such Church records will be found original wills (or copies) filed according to date of probate. In some cases 'Probate Act Books' may be available in which are entered all the probates granted. For some periods, too, there may be volumes of 'registered copies', i.e., volumes in which the wills have been transcribed in full as each was proved, often with the probate act following it. Practically the whole period for which wills are extant in the Prerogative courts is covered by such registered copies bound up in large volumes.

Where there was no will or some irregularity in it, letters of administration, commonly abbreviated to 'admons.', were granted, as they are today. The bonds entered into by the administrators may be found available in some cases and, just as for probates, there may be an (Admon.) Act Book. Admon. may be granted with the will annexed, if, for example, no executor is named or the executor has renounced or died before completing distribution of the estate.

With both proved wills and admons. it will often be found, particularly in the earlier cases, that an inventory is filed with the papers; sometimes an inventory may be there and the will missing, but the admon. may be endorsed on the inventory. The gaps in wills are many, but one must remember that there was not the necessity in the 16th and 17th centuries for a will that there is now. Many were tenants of a manor, so had no real estate to dispose of: there were none of the registered securities that there are today, which need proof of title before a transfer can be made. Property was mostly portable and no doubt the family divided the farm stock, furniture, etc., according to the known wishes of the deceased or by mutual agreement between themselves. In early days there was little means of investment for cash, except perhaps money lent on a bond, so pecuniary legacies were few.

There are printed indexes to many of the wills proved in the pre-1858 probate courts, and others have MS or typescript indexes, in bound volumes or card indexes (often now available on microfilm or fiche). Nearly all of these can be seen on microfilm at the Society of Genealogists' Library. An essential guide through the maze of overlapping probate courts is *Probate jurisdictions: where to look for wills* by J. Gibson (4th ed. 1994). This is arranged by county and within each county by the various probate courts and record repositories, with details of the present location of wills, period of coverage and existence of indexes.

Having studied this guide to find out which was the court having jurisdiction in the locality concerned, one will have to visit the appropriate repository which will have an index of names and produce the documents. In some cases there will be published lists which can be examined beforehand. It should not be forgotten that if a will cannot be found there may be an admon. (usually listed separately) which may give some information on next of kin.

It is advisable to know the date and place of death of the testator whose will is being searched for. If the place is known the will should be looked for in the indexes of the Bishop's Court of the Diocese, and the relative Archdeacon's Court or, if it appears from the list of 'Peculiars' in the Diocese that one of these may have had jurisdiction, the index of Peculiar Courts should be examined. Failing these, the Prerogative Court list of the Province should be searched, where the will would have been proved if the testator owned property in more than one diocese. Wills proved during the Commonwealth whilst the authority of the Ecclesiastical Courts was suspended will be found with P.C.C. wills.

In the case of wills proved since 1858 (when the Court of Probate was established), a search should be made in the Principal Probate Registry indexes at Somerset House, Strand, London WC2R 1LP (tel. 0171 936 6000), which is open to searchers Monday-Friday, 10.00-4.30. There is no charge for looking in the indexes, but there is a small charge (currently 25p) for production of the registered copy of a will when the right reference has been found. The indexes are printed and arranged alphabetically for each year, so it is helpful to have an approximate idea of the date of death (always remembering that a will could have been proved in the year after the death, so it is worth searching on for a year or two if the entry does not turn up in the expected year).

In the case of a common surname the searcher should be able to identify the particular will by the Christian name, place of death and other details given in the indexes.

Copies of the indexes are available in some major libraries and in District Probate Registries, and there are microfilm copies for the years 1858-1930, arranged by initial letter of the surname (so far covering surnames beginning with 'A' to 'S' only, and 'S' to 1868) at the Society of Genealogists. From the information given in these, copies of wills may be ordered by post from Somerset House, applications being addressed to the Record Keeper, Correspondence Department.

Something further should also be said about the P.C.C. wills at the P.R.O. These can be seen on microfilm at the Family Records Centre, 1 Myddelton Street, London EC1R 1UW (see page 7 for current opening hours), as well as at the P.R.O. at Kew (see page 52).

There are printed indexes for the years 1383-1700, and also for 1750-1800, but for the remaining periods it will be necessary to consult the MS indexes (PROB 12) in the search room. These are arranged by year, but are not fully alphabetical, with surnames grouped together by their initial letter. Once the required will has been found, the year of probate and the folio number should be noted. The class list volume (PROB 11) will then provide the reference number for the relevant volume of wills: for instance, a will proved in 1587, folio 34, would be found in the volume PROB 11/70 (which includes folio numbers 1-40). The microfilm for the correct volume can then be located and taken to the microfilm reader.

At this point it will be found that there are two sets of numbers on the pages of wills – stamped numbers on every right-hand page, and a handwritten number (Roman numerals in the early volumes) at the top right-hand corner of every 16 pages. This is the folio number referred to in the indexes, and the will required is to be found in the 16 pages following that number, marked by the testator's name in the margin.

P.C.C. Administrations are to be found in a separate series under the reference PROB 6, or PROB 7 for 'special' or 'limited' grants of administration from 1810 onwards only. Inventories survive for some wills, mainly for the period 1666-1730, and there are separate class lists for them.

Photocopies can easily be ordered at the P.R.O. and may be ready on the same day if ordered early enough.

There is one other important category of probate records at the P.R.O., also available on microfilm at the Family Records Centre.

These are the Death Duty Registers, starting in 1796, when duty became payable on estates over a certain value. As this applied to only a small percentage of estates until 1815, not many wills are to be found in these records until after that date, but for the years 1815-58 the index volumes (IR 27) can be a useful way of tracking down a will without having to search the individual indexes to several different probate courts. The registers, with details of the estate and beneficiaries, are under the reference IR 26, and are an invaluable substitute for the original wills for the counties of Somerset and Devon, whose probate records were destroyed in the bombing of Exeter in 1942.

As with parish registers, some difficulty may be experienced in actually reading the will, when it has been tracked down, and this applies as much to the register copies, such as those at the P.R.O., as to the original wills which are usually seen at other record offices. Indeed, the formal legal hand used for the 18th- and early 19th-century registers of P.C.C. wills is often harder to decipher than the handwriting of the 17th century! The booklets referred to in Chapter 5 (see p.19) will be found equally useful for reading wills, and there is a great advantage in obtaining a photocopy, so that the document can be studied at leisure and in comfort, without the embarrassment of having to admit to being unable to make head or tail of it. Even so, there will always be bad handwriting, just as there is today, and in many cases documents have become worn or damaged over the years, so some wills would tax the skill of even an experienced record searcher.

Another problem, usually first encountered with probate records, is the use of Latin, which was commonly used for grants of probate and administration until the 18th century. However, before despair sets in, bear in mind that there is no need to have studied the language at school, as probate grants are of a standard form, and once the basic layout has become familiar it is fairly easy to pick out the relevant details of name, place and date. A grant begins with the word 'Probatum', not used for administrations, but in both cases the grant is expressed as 'admio. [administratio] commissa fuit ... ' followed by the name(s) of the grantee, and their relationship. The sort of words which occur at this point are 'filio', 'fratri', 'sorori', 'patri' (son, brother, sister, father), or the more complicated 'nepoti ex filia' (a grandson by the daughter, i.e. a grandson who is a daughter's son) or 'nepoti ex fratre' (a nephew, son of a brother).

The date is usually written in words, so a knowledge of the Latin words for numerals is valuable, but the year may be in Arabic numerals. In early records the year may be expressed in Roman numerals, but these can be copied down and worked out later on, rather than risk a miscalculation which then throws a whole pedigree into confusion. It should be noted that the last 'i' in Roman figures is written as a 'j', thus viij = 8.

The date, when between 1 January and 24 March (before 1752, see p.22) may be followed by 'juxta &c,' or 'stylo Angl.' These phrases mean that the year was reckoned as beginning on 25 March, and consequently such a reference after (for example) 20 January 1720 would mean 1720/21, 1721 being the modern dating.

There is a useful copy of a grant of administration, with translation, in *Never been here before?* by Jane Cox (P.R.O. Readers' Guide No.4). Other handbooks to help with the Latin are *Basic Approach to Latin for Family Historians* by M. Gandy (1995), *A Latin Glossary for Family and Local Historians* by J. Morris (1989, reprinted 1995), and the larger but more comprehensive *Latin for Local and Family Historians* by D. Stuart (1995).

The amount of information obtainable from wills varies considerably. In some of the more ancient ones the testator sometimes aggravatingly refers to relationships without giving names, or to 'kinsmen' without giving relationship. He may leave everything to one person or make the genealogist rub his hands with glee by mentioning all the members of a large family including 'his sisters, his cousins and his aunts'. One would naturally search first for the family name but almost equally important may be the wills of 'in-laws' – a father-in-law or mother-in-law (being a widow), may well leave property to the family and particularly mention grandchildren (bear in mind that 'father-in-law' may mean 'step-father'). Uncles and aunts, too, may mention their nephews and nieces, great-nephews and great-nieces. The names of families allied by marriage should be noted for this purpose.

In the will on p.30 Ann Penton and Elizabeth Jestis are daughters and their children named George and Peter respectively are entered in the pedigree (see pp.128-9). Their line is not pursued as they have left the Willis family and name.

One must not forget that until the Married Women's Property Act of 1882 (45 and 46 Vic.c.75) the property of a married woman was with some exceptions, such as property held under a settlement, that of her husband, and that, therefore, if she predeceased her husband she could normally leave no will. Once she was widowed, she could, of course, dispose of property.

When a will required has been found, an abstract of it should be made on a separate sheet for filing as suggested in Chapter 2. The following information should always be noted:

Record Office or other repository where the will was seen, whether it was the original or a copy, and the repository's reference number

Name of testator

Occupation and/or address (in old wills probably only the parish), if given

Date when the will was made

Place of burial desired (this may indicate a family move)

Names and relationship of all beneficiaries

Particulars of all landed estate mentioned

Names of executors, supervisors and overseers (if any)

Names of witnesses

Particulars of heraldic seal (if any)

Date and place of probate

In individual cases there may be some special mention which should be recorded. For instance, the articles bequeathed may be of family interest though not material evidence genealogically. It may be mentioned that it is common in a will to see a legacy of one shilling (see plate 5, p.30). This is not an example of the popular phrase 'cut him off with a shilling'. It is usually included to indicate that the individual is not forgotten, where he has had his portion, perhaps, in the testator's lifetime.

Nor must it be assumed where administration is granted to a creditor, the widow renouncing, that the testator was necessarily bankrupt. It may be merely a means of preventing a rush of small creditors who would eat up the estate. It must not be forgotten that a will reflects conditions at the time of its execution, not at the time of death. If some years have elapsed, children born in the interval will not be mentioned by name (though the possibility of their birth may be provided for in anticipation). Legatees, too, or others mentioned in the will may have predeceased the testator.

The possibilities of parish records, census returns and wills, the leading sources, being exhausted, one must consider the great variety of other sources which might help, and decide which is the most likely. Firstly, there are other classes of ecclesiastical records which give genealogical information, and should be considered next, before turning to national and local records in the Public Record Office and other libraries and record offices.

The relevance of the various sources suggested will, of course, depend on the occupation and status of the family concerned, so, before plunging in, it is worth deciding which is the most likely to be of use.

CHAPTER 8

# Other Ecclesiastical Records

The subject of parish registers and the bishops' transcripts, the best known of ecclesiastical records, has already been discussed in Chapter 5, as one can hardly touch genealogy without them. Other parochial records have been mentioned in Chapter 6. But there are a number of other sources of genealogical value amongst what might be called regional ecclesiastical archives.

The hierarchy of the established Church of England now consists of the two archbishops, the diocesan bishops with assistant or suffragan bishops, archdeacons, rural deans and parochial clergy. Except for rural deans, who do not seem to have any ancient records, and the assistant and suffragan bishops, each of these categories has archives representing the work of their predecessors. The archives of diocesan bishops were in the charge of their Diocesan Registrar and those of archdeacons were with their 'Official', usually a solicitor having a relation to the archdeacon like that of the Registrar to the bishop. In a different category is the Dean or Provost of a cathedral. He and the Canons who form the Chapter are responsible for the maintenance and services of the Cathedral and are not part of the episcopal administration authorities. The archives of the Dean and Chapter will normally be found in the Cathedral Library.

In recent years there has been a tendency towards transfer of episcopal and archdeacons' ancient records from the official custodian who is busy with current work to such a repository as a county or municipal record office, where there is an expert staff for cataloguing and repair and proper storage accommodation, but some are still with Diocesan Registrars.

Overint Univerſi per præſentes; Nos *John Willis de Emersley in Com Southton Pipemaker, et Roger: pond de Emersley for Pipemaker teneri & firmiter Obligari Rev: in Chriſto Patri ac Dno Dno Jonathan &c Divina Winton Epo* in *Do: Anglibris bonæ & legalis Monetæ Magnæ Britaniæ, ſolvend' eidem R &c 9br: — aut ſuo certo Attornato, Executoribus, Adminiſtratoribus, vel aſſignatis ſuis: Ad quam quidem ſolutionem bene & fideliter faciend' Obligamus Nos & utrumque noſtrum per ſe pro toto & in ſolido, Hæredes, Executores, & Adminiſtratores noſtros firmiter per præſentes. Sigillis noſtris Sigillat' Dat'* Decimo Sophimo *dis menſis May Anno Regni Dni nri Georgy Dei gra: Mag: Brit: Franciæ & Hibniæ Regis &c Defenſ &c quarto Annoq; Dni 1718°*

THE Condition of this Obligation is ſuch, That if there ſhall not hereafter appear any Lawful Lett or Impediment, by Reaſon of any Pre-contract, Conſanguinity, Affinity, or any other juſt Cauſe whatſoever; but that *the above bounden John Willis a Batchelour and Mary Marchant of Emersley aforeſd Spinſter*

———————————————————————————

may lawfully Marry together, and that there is not any Suit depending before any Judge Eccleſiaſtical or Civil, for, or concerning any ſuch Pre-contract: And that the Conſent of the Parents, or others the Governours of the ſaid Parties, be thereunto firſt had and obtain'd. And that they cauſe their ſaid Marriage to be openly ſolemniz'd in the Face of the Pariſh Church of *St Thomas in the Citty of Winchoſter* between the Hours of Eight and Twelve of the Clock in the Forenoon: And do and ſhall ſave harmleſs, and keep Indemnified the above-nam'd *Lord Biſhop his Chancellor and* — his Surrogates, and all other his Officers, and Succeſſors in Office, for and concerning the Premiſes; That then this Obligation to be void and of none effect, or elſe to remain in full force and vertue.

Signat' Sigillat', & Deliberat'
in præſentia.

*Chris Dawkins*          *John Willis*
                         *Roger pond*

**Plate 7**   *A Marriage Allegation Bond (from the Records of the Diocesan Registrar, Winchester).
(Reproduced by courtesy of the Hampshire Record Office.)*

## Marriage Licences

One of the most valuable items for the genealogist is the set of marriage licence 'allegations'. These are the documents on which the licences were issued and consist of an affidavit supported by a bond (the bond was discontinued in 1823–4 Geo.IV, c.76, section 15). See plate 7, p.44.

The affidavit is normally by one of the parties, often giving his trade or occupation, declaring that there is no lawful impediment by consanguinity or other cause. It may state the age of each party (valuable for tracing baptism record) or simply declare that they are over twenty-one. Where either of the parties is under 21, the consent of parent or guardian may be endorsed or be in a separate document, so giving valuable genealogical evidence. The affidavit will also state the church in which the marriage is to be solemnized, a pointer to the parish register for the entry.

The bond is given by two sureties, one normally being one of the parties. It vouches that there is no impediment to the marriage. The bondsman's name is sometimes useful, being that of perhaps a father or brother.

A large proportion of these marriage licence records have been printed and indexed, particularly by the Harleian Society and the British Record Society, and also by local societies and individuals. For further details on the location of original records and indexes, reference should be made to *Bishop's Transcripts and Marriage Licences, Bonds and Allegations: Guide to their Location and Indexes*, by J. Gibson (3rd ed. 1991), which also details the dates for which these records survive in the different dioceses.

## Wills and Administrations

Though the ecclesiastical authorities should have handed over all testamentary papers to the Probate Registry when it was formed in 1858, many were apparently retained. This was in small part due to probate matter being in the same registers as the marriage licences just mentioned, but there was, for example, at Winchester a very substantial collection, probably remaining because the first Probate Registrar in 1858 was the Diocesan Registrar himself. Having both offices at that time in the same building, he no doubt did no moving about of the records and they were evidently moved away with the diocesan records when he left the building. The list of these, now with the County Archivist, has been published. (*Wills, Administrations and Inventories with the Winchester Diocesan Records*, A.J. Willis (1968).)

## Court Papers

The ecclesiastical courts, besides having jurisdiction over testamentary matters, heard many disputes about tithes, actions of defamation (slander), matrimonial disputes and sexual offences and various causes of a disciplinary nature arising from behaviour of churchwardens or other officials, disputes about seating, etc. Testamentary causes will, of course, quite often give information about relationships, but the others may not give much but biographical information, except for one important category.

As in the Court of Chancery, so in the ecclesiastical courts evidence was taken by deposition, and the deponent gave his place of birth, age, and previous places of residence. The value of these records to the genealogist will depend very largely on whether they have been indexed. It should be mentioned that (as with most evidence of age) one must use the age given with allowance made for a margin both ways. Ages sometimes seem to be given to the nearest five years, and, no doubt, there were occasions when the deponent did not know with any accuracy.

There was one thing which, though nominally a matter for the bishop's court, was probably largely administrative in character, viz. the appointment of guardians for minors. This mostly arose when a minor on the death of his parents wanted to prove a will, but was not able to do so because of his status. The

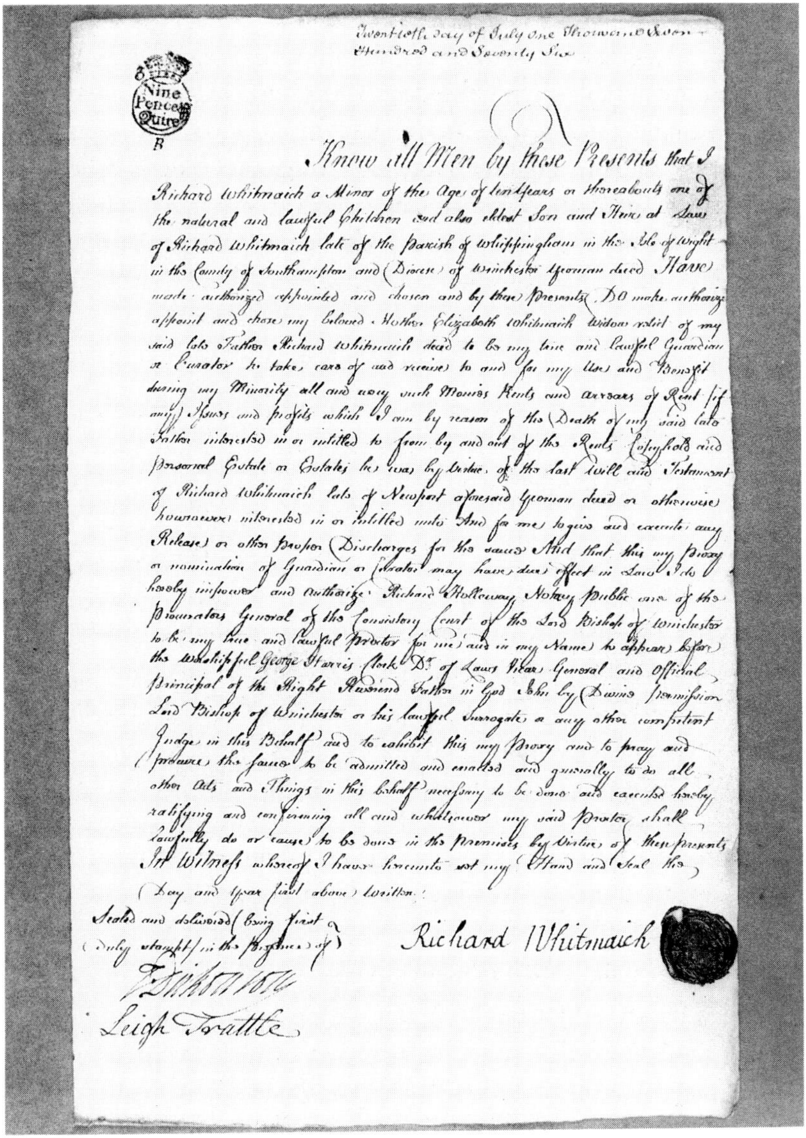

**Plate 8** *A Guardianship Appointment.*
*(Reproduced by courtesy of the Hampshire Record Office.)*

Court appointed somebody, usually a near relation, to act on his behalf. Two documents are found, the appointment of the guardian by name, signed and sealed by the minor (if under the age of seven, and so an 'infant', the deed was signed by a near relative on his behalf), and the Act of Court making the appointment signed by the Vicar General or his Surrogate. Sometimes several brothers and sisters are covered by the same deed. As the names and ages of the minors are given, as well as the names and parish of their parents and of the guardian (often with his relationship), these documents are of great value to genealogists (see plate 8).

At Winchester all these Court papers are indexed in typescript, copies being available both at the Society of Genealogists' Library and at Winchester, so that any name can be turned up in a few minutes, but the same indexing may not be found in other dioceses. A calendar of these guardianship papers has been published. (*Winchester Guardianships after 1700*, A.J. Willis (1967).)

## Clergy

Anyone interested in the clergy genealogically should not omit to look at the episcopal records, which include, of course, much about them. They will contain the administrative archives of ordination, licence to curacies, presentation and institution or collation to livings, nominations to perpetual curacies, non-residence licences, resignations and sequestrations. There may also be caveats against ordination. With the archdeacon's records should be induction mandates.

The most important of these for genealogists are the ordination papers, because they should contain a baptismal or birth certificate. Unfortunately this is sometimes missing, but, if not found with the papers for ordination as deacon, it may be with those for ordination as priest. Apparently both this certificate and testimonials were required on both occasions. The testimonial for deacon's orders will probably be from the college of the ordinand's university, signed by the head and principal fellows. It will give his degree and sometimes mention that he was a scholar or is a fellow of the college. The testimonial for priests' orders is often signed by three neighbouring clergy. Other records of ordination may be found in other places, but not with this detail. The Bishop's Register (a volume recording his official acts) lists the names at each ordination, usually with their degrees and sometimes their college. There may be an ordination register extant for the period with the archives, and the earlier Visitation Books record the production of orders at the first visitation of a bishop after his consecration. These are often useful to show a move, as they mention date and ordaining bishop for both deacon's and priest's orders, the latter often being in a different diocese from the former.

The other papers referred to above will show movements of the clergy from curacy to curacy or living, and again there may be registers giving this information as well.

The 'Subscription Books' should be mentioned, as these contain the declarations of ordinands of adherence to the Thirty-nine Articles and other requirements of Canon 36 of 1603 and of conformity to the Liturgy of the Church of England. Similar declarations were required on institution to a benefice or licence to a curacy together with a declaration against simony. The extent to which these books have survived will vary in different dioceses, but they are valuable for the signatures of the clergy.

### Licences to Laymen*

*See Bishops' Licences to Laymen in the 18th and 19th Centuries, Arthur J. Willis. The Amateur Historian, vol.5, no.1.

The Church was interested in education long before the State took notice of it and, no doubt, as the duties were handed over to laymen the appointments were subject to licence by the bishop. The Church, too, has long been interested in the welfare of the body as well as the soul and still is, as will be seen by their support of medical missions. Physicians, surgeons and midwives were all licensed by the bishop. These licences extend through the 18th century and those for schoolmasters well into the nineteenth.

The value to the genealogist of this licensing is that testimonials were submitted and these give information as to where schoolmasters were teaching and to whom physicians and surgeons were apprenticed (sometimes to their father).

Parish clerks and sextons also were licensed by the bishop and produced testimonials.

## *Records of Papists and Dissenters*

Returns of papists from each parish may be found. Though sometimes these are only statistics, there may be lists of names.

Following the Toleration Act of 1688 (1 W.&M., c.18) dissenters were required to apply to the bishop of the diocese or the sessions to have their meeting houses licensed. Applications will give name of owner or occupier of the premises and possibly have other supporters' signatures.

Discovery of the wanted name in either of these categories would turn the searcher to Roman Catholic records, such as those of the Catholic Record Society or to Non-conformist records, such as the non-parochial registers (see pp.24-5).

## *Manorial Records*

Bishops were in the past large landowners and if an ancestor was in a place found to be within an episcopal manor, the manorial records should be sought out. Manorial records generally are considered in Chapter 12 (page 73).

Wherever the manorial records may be, there may be remaining in the Diocesan Registry or other repository something of the manorial papers or other deeds and records relating to land.

## *Other Records*

There will certainly be other records which will vary from diocese to diocese, probably more of historical than genealogical interest. Such would be visitorship documents (arising from the bishop's position as Visitor to a College), replies from the parishes to Visitation Inquiries, consecration and faculty papers, surrogates' bonds, Registrars' accounts, general correspondence, etc.

# CHAPTER 9

# The Public Record Office

The Public Record Office is the repository of official records of the Courts of Law and of the Departments of State. For the genealogist it is only in so far as his quarry has come into contact with such official bodies that he will find mention of him there. If he was involved in legal proceedings, or, as a member of the Navy or Army or otherwise, was of interest to a Government Department, there may be information about him in the Public Records. Taxation may have brought him to the notice of the Exchequer or transfer of landed property to the Court of Chancery.

The mass of material is enormous, and only a few of the more obvious and important sources of information will be mentioned. These will probably be the first to be investigated unless a definite clue leads elsewhere. If so, its particular direction should be followed; unless there is some such guidance the searcher may find himself lost in a maze of lists, indexes and calendars if he strays beyond the few recognised sources of genealogical information. (See *Tracing your Ancestors in the Public Record Office* by J. Cox and T. Padfield, revised by A. Bevan and A. Duncan (4th ed., 3rd impression, 1992).) An examination of the *Guide to the Contents of the Public Record Office* will give an idea of the immense variety of material. To take just two items, a very small bite out of the whole, there are 17,471 volumes of Ships' Musters for the period 1688-1808 in the Admiralty records and 13,305 volumes of Muster Books (General) amongst the War Office records.

The Public Record Office is now based in Kew, where the address is Ruskin Avenue, Kew, Richmond, Surrey TW9 4DU (tel. 0181 876 3444), having left its historic Chancery Lane premises in 1996. However, certain classes of records of particular interest to genealogists are still available on microfilm in central London; these are the Census Returns, P.C.C. Wills, Death Duty Registers and Nonconformist Registers. In addition, microfilms of the P.C.C. Wills only can be seen at Kew. The London address for these records is the Family Records Centre, 1 Myddelton Street, London EC1R 1UW. All of these sources are described more fully in Chapters 4, 5 and 7.

The P.R.O. is open Monday to Friday, 9.30-5.00, except the usual public holidays and two weeks closure for stock-taking in early October. The nearest station is Kew Gardens, a 10-minute walk away, and there are also several bus routes nearby and ample space for car-parking. A useful map and information leaflet can be obtained in advance by post.

There is no charge for searching the records, but a reader's ticket must be obtained at the shop in the foyer, which will be issued on production of some means of identification, such as a banker's card, driving licence or passport.

The ground floor of the P.R.O. consists of a vast foyer, reminiscent of an airport lounge, with a well-stocked and most useful bookshop, cloakrooms and a restaurant. The main search rooms (Langdale Room and Romilly Room) and the Reference Room are on the first floor, with the Map Room on the second floor, for reading maps and other large documents.

All this is most helpfully explained and amplified in a beginner's guide to the P.R.O.: *Never Been Here Before?* by Jane Cox (1993), a 'must' for anyone new to the building and its records, and excellent value for money.

Documents are ordered by computer in the Reference Room, using the reader's ticket and a 'bleeper' (from the long counter in the main search room), which has a seat number on it. All the necessary lists, indexes and reference books, with explanatory information, can be found in the Reference Room, but before attempting to use them the reader should select the relevant free leaflets which are in the lobby on the first floor and give advice on what material is available on various topics, and how to use the indexes or class lists. Anyone who still feels completely at sea will find the staff most helpful and sympathetic.

Having ordered the documents required, one can browse in the bookshop, or perhaps have coffee or a meal at the restaurant, or eat one's own sandwich in the foyer or outside, while waiting for the bleeper to bleep. This indicates that the documents are ready for collection at the desk in the search room. In some cases, there may be no wait at all, as documents on microfilm can be seen at once in the Romilly Room.

The following are the classes of record most likely to be of interest to the genealogist.

## Armed Forces and Other Service Records

### Army

For officers, there are printed Army Lists from 1754 (WO 65-66), and MS lists from 1702 (WO 64). Some of these can, of course, be seen in other libraries, but the P.R.O. series will be more complete. Muster Books (WO 10-15), which begin in 1708, list both officers and other ranks by regiment and were used for day-to-day administration of the regiment; the first entry for a new recruit usually gives his age, place of enlistment and trade. Other main classes of record are Soldiers' Documents (discharge papers), 1760-1913 (WO 97) for soldiers discharged to pension, and Description and Depot Books, 1778-1908 (WO 25 and 67). These should give details of place of birth and career.

It really is essential to know the regiment before attempting to search any of these records, and while the Army Lists provide this information for officers, other sources have to be used for other ranks, in the absence of any family information on the subject.

Beware of the often repeated legend of the ancestor who fought at Waterloo, as this can lead to fruitless hours toiling through Muster Books of all the regiments who were there, only to discover elsewhere that the soldier in question was serving on quite a different front.

The P.R.O. produces an Information Leaflet *Sources for Military Genealogy and Biography* and two Family Fact Sheets on *Tracing an Ancestor in the Army: Soldiers* and *Officers* which should be consulted for more detailed advice.

For an ancestor who served in a local militia regiment, there are the Militia Attestation papers, 1806-1915 (WO 96) and the Militia Records, 1759-1925 (WO 68), which should provide details of date and place of birth, and career.

### Navy

As with the army, there are printed Navy Lists for officers from 1782, from which the details of a man's career can be discovered. Information on officers can also be found in Lieutenants' Passing Certificates, 1691-1848 (ADM 107), which include a copy of the baptism certificate, and officers' service records from 1756 (ADM 196).

For tracing a rating the name of his ship must be known in order to find him in Ships' Musters, 1688-1878 (ADM 36-41) and Ships' Pay Books, 1691-1856 (ADM31-35). There are records of seamen's pensions, 1802-1919 (ADM 29), Continuous Service Engagement Books, 1853-1872 (ADM 139) and Seamen's services, 1837-1891 (ADM 188), which provide more information.

There are also a great many seamen's wills and grants of administration, for ordinary sailors as well as officers, from 1786 onwards (ADM 42, 44 and 45); in addition, P.C.C. wills include many wills for seamen, and, as already mentioned, can be seen on microfilm at the P.R.O.

There are Family Fact Sheets available at the P.R.O., similar to those for army records: *Tracing an Ancestor in the Royal Navy:*

*Ratings* and *Officers*, as well as the Information Leaflet *Admiralty Records as Sources for Biography and Genealogy*.

## Royal Marines

The Marines were established in 1755, but there are no separate records back to that date. Officers are included in the Navy Lists and their records are included with those of naval officers in the class ADM 196. Other ranks can be traced through Attestations Papers (discharge documents), 1790-1901 (ADM 157) and service records, 1884-1918 (ADM 313 and 159). Once again, there is an Information Leaflet, *Royal Marines Records in the Public Record Office*.

## Merchant Seamen

Until 1853 the details of a merchant seaman's service may be, at least in part, with naval records, as described above, since the same men switched between the services as the situation required.

There are registers of seamen 1835-1844 (BT 112), and also registers of seamen's tickets, 1845-1853 (BT 113), but the registration of seamen stopped in 1857, and after that date there is no easy way of tracing them, although some may appear in the records of the Royal Naval Reserve established in 1859 (ADM 240 and BT 164).

If the name of a seaman's ship or port is known, it may be worth searching crew lists, 1747-1860 (BT 98), and there are also records of apprentices in the merchant fleet, 1824-1953 (BT 150).

The relevant Family Fact Sheets are *Tracing an Ancestor in the Merchant Navy: Seamen* and *Masters and Mates*, while there is also an Information Leaflet, *Records of the Register General of Shipping and Seamen*.

## Other Services

Service records of other occupations which came under various government departments are also to be found at the P.R.O. These include Coastguards (from 1822), Customs and Excise Officers (from 1820), Dockyard workers (from 1660), Railway Company employees, Metropolitan Police officers (from 1829) and members of the Royal Irish Constabulary (from 1836).

The quantity and quality of records varies from one class to another, but there are Family Fact Sheets and Information Leaflets available with more details on each of the above services, and others.

## Professional Records

**Solicitors and Attorneys**

While records of barristers are not at the P.R.O. (The Inns of Court should be consulted here), there are some documents relating to solicitors and attorneys. These are the Attorneys' and Solicitors' Rolls or Books, which begin in 1729, recording the names of those about to serve their five years as clerks under articles, followed by the Affidavits of Due Execution of Articles of Clerkship, beginning in 1749, which mark the end of that period of training. Further details can be found in the Information Leaflet *Records of Attorneys and Solicitors in the Public Record Office.*

## Naturalisation Certificates

These records, granted to immigrants wishing to become naturalised subjects, begin in 1844 and are in classes HO 1 and HO 334. Prior to that date, denization was more frequent, being less expensive, and denizations were enrolled on Patent Rolls (C 66 and C67). Indexes to these, 1509-1800 and 1801-1873, are attached to the list of HO 1. However, most foreign settlers did not bother with these formalities, so cannot be traced through these records.

## Apprenticeship Books

Between 1710 and 1811, apprenticeship indentures were subject to tax, and thus records of them are at the P.R.O. (IR 1, indexed in IR 17). These books record the names, addresses and trades of the masters, and the name of the apprentices, with the date of the indenture; their parents' names are given up to 1752. There are indexes to these records (covering apprentices 1710-1774 and masters 1710-1762) at the Society of Genealogists, and further indexes are in preparation.

## Lay Subsidies

Among Exchequer records are the Subsidy Rolls, which include assessments and accounts for various grants made to the Crown, by Convocation for the clergy, and by the House of Commons for the laity. The latter, the 'lay subsidies', extend up to the reign of Charles II, and are useful to genealogists as they give the names of those who were assessed for taxation, arranged by villages within each hundred (an area of local administration) of every county.

The most useful for the genealogist are the hearth tax returns and assessments of 1662-1674 (E 179), the most complete being those for 1664. Some earlier tax returns include names, and this is noted in the class list.

Also of interest are the Land Tax Redemption Office Quotas and Assessments (IR 23), which list all owners of property subject to tax in England and Wales, 1798-1799, arranged by parish. In 1798 this tax became a fixed annual charge and many people purchased exemption; these records sometimes include maps and plans (IR 22 and 24).

There is an Information Leaflet, *Taxation Records as a Source for Local and Family History*.

## Inquisitions Post Mortem

On the death of a tenant in chief of the Crown, an enquiry was held before a jury, who had to swear to the lands held by the tenant, and the name, age and relationship of the next heir; this process continued up to 1660, when feudal tenures were abolished. The records of these inquisitions are among Chancery, Exchequer and Court of Wards records, and are indexed. They are, however, of little relevance except in the case of substantial landowning families.

## Feet of Fines

When conveyance of landed property was in a very rudimentary stage somebody seems to have discovered that if there could be a dispute at law about the ownership of land, and that dispute was settled by the Court, first-class evidence as to ownership was thereby provided. Hence, it seems, arose the series of 'Fines' (so-called because they made a final end to the dispute, the general opening to the Foot of Fine being '*Hec est finalis concordia* ...'). The 'Fine' was an agreement or composition of a suit (usually fictitious) made between the parties with the consent of the Court and by which the transfer or settlement of freehold property was determined. There were several steps in the procedure, but the 'Foot of Fine' set out the terms of the agreement. For an example see p.92. Where several members of the same family were concerned, their relationship would normally be given. Feet of Fines are in Latin until the reign of George II, after which they are in English, and continue until 1833.

Some indexes and calendars to Feet of Fines have been published by various local societies, and these are the easiest means of reference. There is a useful article on the subject, 'Feet of Fines', by M. Tatchell (*Genealogists' Magazine*, vol.19, no.10, June 1979, pp.347-9).

## Law Court Records

The records of the various law courts are to be found at the P.R.O., so, if the family has been known to have engaged in a lawsuit, information may be found there in the form of affidavits lodged and judgements, with other papers such as private deeds. However, searching all these classes of records is a lengthy process, and is not something to be undertaken on the offchance that something might turn up, unless all other avenues have drawn a blank, and even then only if the family concerned was reasonably prosperous and likely to have engaged in a lawsuit. Among Law Court Records, the following should be specially mentioned.

## Chancery Proceedings

A good deal of litigation, largely in relation to property or money, came before the Equity side of the Court of Chancery in the form of petitions (or 'bills'), with their answers and depositions. Calendars of the early suits have been printed, but for later ones only MS calendars are available. These are classified under the names of the Six Clerks, and up to 1714 give bundle reference number, names of plaintiffs and defendants, date and subject matter of the suit, and name of the county concerned. These particulars are grouped together under the initial letter of the principal plaintiff's name, and one may therefore find a suit where this is known. But it is not so easy to trace the name of a defendant or associated plaintiff. It is, of course, necessary to search the lists of all the Six Clerks, unless it is known by which the suit was handled. In cases where several members of the same family are either joint or opposite parties, relationship may be established from these suits. After 1714 the lists give names of parties only without any county, so the help of locality in eliminating the unwanted is not available. A further problem is that papers dealing with a single case are not filed together, but with other documents of the same type from different cases, so it is very difficult to follow through one particular suit.

The value to genealogists of these proceedings is, however, not so much in the bills and answers as in the depositions of witnesses which are filed with the papers. The deponents give their age and place of residence and sometimes other genealogical information. For names in these the Bernau Index, on microfilm at the Society of Genealogists (see Chapter 10), is worth consulting, as it includes names in Chancery Proceedings 1714-1800, two series of Depositions and parts of other classes of records.

While on the subject of Chancery, many families have stories of untold millions awaiting a claimant 'in Chancery'. It is true that since 1876 solicitors have deposited money for which they were unable to trace legatees or next of kin, and lists of these have been published as supplements to the *London Gazette* from 1893, which can be consulted at the P.R.O. However, successful claims to one of these funds are extremely rare, and the sums of money involved are mostly very insignificant.

**Exchequer Depositions**
Similar depositions to those in Chancery are found in the Court of Exchequer records. There is a printed calendar and here supplementary information is available to trace deponents, with a typed list of deponents in each case for the period 1559-1695, the cases being arranged in groups according to locality, with the county given in a marginal heading. This is also available at the Society of Genealogists, with MS slips for the later period up to 1800.

Useful guides to these legal records are *Chancery and other Legal Proceedings* by R.E.F. Garrett (Shalfleet Manor 1968), the Information Leaflet *An Introduction to Chancery Proceedings* and an article, 'Genealogical Resources in Chancery Records', P.W. Coldham (*Genealogists' Magazine*, vol.XIX, pp.345-57 and vol.XX, pp.257-60).

\* \* \*

Some of the items mentioned above are approaching more advanced work, but it seems advisable to draw attention to their existence. The main interest of the beginner at the P.R.O. will be in the records of the armed forces and other government employees and perhaps Apprenticeship Books, in addition to those records which can be consulted in central London and are the basis for most genealogical research.

There are, however, public records elsewhere, such as county and municipal archives, as well as a very large number of printed sources and transcriptions of original records, all of which can provide vital clues for family history.

There are also other important repositories for genealogists, such as the Library of the Society of Genealogists, for both national and local material, and county or city libraries for items of local interest. Next, therefore, must be examined the resources of libraries, which will cover not only manuscripts but the vast collections of printed books available.

CHAPTER 10

# The Society of Genealogists' Library

This is one of the most important repositories in the country for any genealogist, containing a unique and ever-growing collection of material, much of it available on open shelves. The library is at the Society's headquarters, 14 Charterhouse Buildings, Goswell Road, London EC1M 7BA (tel. 0171 251 8799 or 0171 250 0291 – library only), and is open on Tuesday, Friday and Saturday from 10 a.m. to 6 p.m., and on Wednesday and Thursday until 8 p.m. (closed on Monday). There are regular closures for stock-taking, normally the week of the first Monday in February, and Friday afternoons and Saturdays prior to Bank Holidays, but it is just as well to check this.

Membership of the Society, giving free access to the Library, a quarterly magazine and the opportunity to attend a varied programme of lectures and courses, costs £30 for London members or £21 for country and overseas members, plus an initial Entrance Fee of £7.50. Non-members may also use the Library on payment of a fee (£3 for an hour, £7.50 for four hours or £10 for a day.

In addition, the Society has a well-stocked bookshop selling a wide range of genealogical guides and handbooks, many published by the Society itself. These can also be obtained by post, and a list will be sent on receipt of a stamped addressed envelope.

The Society is unable to carry out research for those who cannot visit the Library, but it will provide the names of searchers who are able to help.

As the majority of the Society's collection relates to the period before civil registration in 1837, it is essential for the prospective visitor to have collected as much information as possible from the General Register Office and census returns, and to have a clear idea of what to look for. A plan of the Library is given free to new members, and the comprehensive guide *Using the Library of the Society of Genealogists*, which can be obtained from the bookshop, is well worth its modest cost.

The following is a brief summary of the principal records and printed sources available in the Society's Library, but obviously it cannot be exhaustive, and, when a series of publications is mentioned, it must not be assumed to be complete. Further details are to be found in the two main catalogues for the Library.

**Regional**

This part of the Library is arranged alphabetically by English counties (as existing in 1837), with separate sections for Wales, Scotland and Ireland. The records include:

Items relating to the whole county, such as histories, bibliographies, maps, newspapers, record office guides and wills

More local items, including parish histories, church guides or other material on particular places

Parish registers: the Society holds the largest collection in the country of copies, printed, typescript, manuscript and on film or fiche (see *Parish Register Copies in the Library of the Society of Genealogists*, 1995)

Monumental Inscriptions, copied from tombstones in countless numbers of churches and churchyards

Census Returns: a constantly expanding collection of indexes to the names in the censuses, 1841-1891, and microfiche of the 1881 Census Transcription project

Trade Directories from the 1770s onwards, and Poll Books (lists of voters at parliamentary elections) between 1694 and 1832

Local collections, being the results of research carried out by former members and including the Snell Collection (Berkshire), the Rogers Collection (Cornwall), the Campling Collection (Norfolk) and Boyd's Inhabitants of London and London Burials.

**Family Histories**
Printed and typescript volumes of family history
Documents relating to particular families (items acquired since 1992 on microfiche)
Manuscript and printed pedigrees
History of surnames
Names of families on which members of the Society are working

**Trades and Professions**
Apprentices of Great Britain: a typescript index to the series of records at the P.R.O. covering the years 1710-1744
Crisp's Apprenticeship Indentures (some original documents bound in two series, 1641-1749 and 1775-1888) and Crisp's Bonds (bound volumes of originals 1590-1847)
School Lists, mainly for public schools
University and College Registers
Army Lists from 1661-1714 and 1740-1987
Navy Lists from 1756 and naval biographical dictionaries
Air Force Lists from 1937
Law Lists, 1813-1973
Records of Admissions to the Inns of Court
Medical Directories and Registers from 1845, and reference books for earlier periods
Trinity House Petitions, 1750-1890: applications for pensions by seamen

**Boyd's Marriage Index**
This is in over 500 bound typescript volumes, and contains entries, arranged alphabetically under men's and (in most cases) women's surnames, compiled from transcribed parish registers available at

the time it was prepared. It is limited to certain English counties and is obviously not complete, but can often provide useful information. The counties covered are: Cambridgeshire, Cornwall, Cumberland (to 1700 only), Derbyshire, Devon, Co. Durham, Essex, Gloucestershire, Lancashire, Middlesex and London, Norfolk, Northumberland, Shropshire, Somerset, Suffolk, Yorkshire. There is also a 'Miscellaneous' section covering some other counties.

**Other Indexes**
Great Card Index. This contains several million slips, arranged by surname with references to various sources, including parish registers, marriage licences, legal records and monumental inscriptions; most surnames are represented, and the Index is a fair guide to their distribution.
Dwelly Index. West Country material
Whitehead Index. East Anglian references
Fawcett Index. Clergy and North Country families
Glencross Index. Separate indexes for surnames and places
Graham Index. Mostly Scottish families
Macleod Collection. Working papers of two Scottish genealogists for several hundred Scottish families

**Indexes on Microfilm and Fiche**
General Register Office. Microfiche copies of the indexes to births, marriages and deaths for England and Wales, 1837-1920
Scottish General Registers Office. Microfilm copies of the indexes to births, marriages and deaths for Scotland, 1855-1920
Scottish Old Parochial Registers. Microfiche indexes to all births, baptisms and marriages in all the Old Parochial Registers 1553-1854
Bernau's Index. A microfilm collection relating to unindexed material in the Chancery and Exchequer Court depositions at the

P.R.O., which includes every litigant in Chancery between 1714 and 1758

## International Genealogical Index

This is described more fully in Chapter 5 (pp.17-18). The Society possesses the most recently available edition and also has the Index for the whole world on CD-ROM.

The Library also has collections of material relating to families in America, India, the West Indies, Australia, New Zealand and Canada, as well as a comprehensive collection of reference books on genealogy, heraldry, the peerage and royalty, biographical dictionaries, and various genealogical periodicals. The journals of various specialist societies are also available, including those of the Harleian Society, Jewish Historical Society and the Society of Friends.

While there is normally no need to telephone in advance before visiting the Library, it is advisable if intending to use material on microfilm or microfiche, in order to book a reader, as these are much in demand.

# CHAPTER 11

# Other Libraries

O ther libraries will vary considerably in size and scope. There are general libraries such as the British Library, the Bodleian at Oxford, or the Cambridge University Library, and local libraries in each city or borough, the larger of which, whil•et having a special section of local books, approximate to a general library. There are also specialist libraries such as those of learned societies like the Society of Antiquaries, certain Government Departments with special spheres of administration or County Record Offices which will concentrate on books relating to the particular county. Some will even have a general genealogical collection, as in Manchester whose Public Library has published a catalogue of their genealogical books in three volumes. This is a very useful reference book, giving, for instance, a list of the parishes covered by the Phillimore series of printed parish registers in each county. County, city and borough reference libraries are free, but the libraries of societies are mostly restricted to their members, though facilities will usually be allowed to research students with or without payment of a fee.

Apart from the specific requirement of the Copyright Act for delivery of a copy of every publication to the British Library, certain other libraries have under various enactments been entitled to claim a copy. A clause in the Copyright Act of 1911 (unrepealed by the Act of 1956) requires delivery on request of a copy of every publication to the Bodleian Library, the Cambridge University Library, the National Libraries of Scotland and Wales, and the Library of Trinity College, Dublin. Such a request is, in fact, mostly

made, and in any case publishers often send copies automatically
without waiting for a request, so these libraries should have all
British publications of value to genealogists, at any rate since 1911.
One must naturally adapt one's use of a library to the particular
case in hand. It is no use looking at old numbers of *Landed Gentry*
or *The Gentleman's Magazine* when dealing with a working man's
family; on the other hand, a directory or local newspaper might
in such a case be useful. One must investigate to see what can be
found in a general library rather than expect to be told what to
look for.

The genealogist should make a point of visiting public reference
libraries in his neighbourhood. He may quite possibly find material
which he can study more conveniently than by paying a visit to
London. For instance, the library in a county town may well have
microfilm copies of local census returns, and indexes, a copy of
the International Genealogical Index for the county or even for
the whole country and printed copies of local parish registers.

An examination of the lending library section may provide
something interesting. The reference for books on genealogy,
following the decimal classification commonly used by libraries,
is 929, so the relative books can quickly found. Most reference
libraries have a classified index, often on microfiche, and the
section on Genealogy might be looked through, as some books
may be out on loan and so not seen on the shelves. Whilst such
searching in a public library will most likely not produce an answer
to the immediate genealogical quest, it widens one's knowledge
of the possibilities and so indirectly is a help. Without a knowledge
of the contents of all the main libraries one cannot give any general
guide, but one or two categories might be mentioned.

## *A City or Borough Library*

In any big municipal library will be found all the reference books
of a general nature likely to be required, e.g., *Dictionary of National*

*Biography*, atlases and gazetteers, standard histories, etc. One item which may be useful is the index to *The Times*. At Westminster City Library, for instance, this is available back to 1855; at Guildhall in the City of London it goes back to 1791. This may be of little help to the genealogist in Manchester or Sheffield. He should make a point of investigating his own local libraries. He is certain to find something of interest.

A public library, particularly that of a county town or other large centre, is fairly certain to have a good collection of topographical literature on its own district. It may be worthwhile paying a special visit to the library of a district in which lived the family being traced. Not only may there be books of local interest, perhaps privately printed or otherwise rare, but there may sometimes be manuscript records to be found. The public library in a large town may have a separate department of archives holding collections of the papers of local families as well as, possibly, deposited parish records. Though one may not be searching for gentry, some member of such families as a magistrate or churchwarden may have retained or acquired a collection of documents bearing on his duties. Recently in Sheffield a long list of apprenticeships and a list of poor-law papers have been prepared from such a source.

Finally, a borough library may well have the records of the meetings of various bodies which administered the borough, the rolls of its freemen and accounts of its financial officers. The borough may have supervised the placing of apprentices in which case there may be apprenticeship records.

## *Guildhall Library*

Guildhall Library in the City of London deserves special mention as one of the principal city libraries and with some material of more than local interest.

The Library does not make any charge, nor is there any need for a reader's ticket, and it is open on Saturdays, unlike most record offices. The archives include records of the Freemen of the City of London and of the City Livery Companies, including apprenticeship and admissions registers. It is worth remembering that before the 19th century all who practised a trade or craft within the City had to be both Livery Company members and Freemen. However, many Freemen who did not work in the City were not Livery Company members, so they may only appear in one set of records. Furthermore, many liverymen had their origins outside London (Dick Whittington being the most famous example), and a father's place of residence is often given in apprenticeship books, which can provide a vital clue.

The Library also holds the original registers of virtually every City parish, and also wills proved in the Archdeaconry and Commissary Courts of London, as well as many London marriage licence allegations.

In addition, there are comprehensive collections of Directories and Poll Books and, of course, a huge collection of printed and MS material relating to the City of London, including letters and other private papers and matters concerning ceremonial and the City Corporation.

## County Record Offices

County record offices will mainly be used for their collections of parish registers, wills and bishops' transcripts and marriage licence allegations, as well as maps, manorial records, estate records, old photographs and family papers.

In addition, the records of the local county authority will be in the county record office. One important category of records which may be found there are the order books and other records of the Courts of Quarter Sessions for the county. These might be either of the full Court sitting four times a year or of the country magistrates who were empowered to make orders to a limited extent. Besides a restricted jurisdiction in criminal cases, the Quarter Sessions exercised a kind of supervision over local

administration before the days of the County Councils, County
Courts or the Local Government Board. Hence came before it
such matters as bastardy cases, breaches of apprenticeship
indentures and disputes over parish settlement (see pp.27), all of
which may yield genealogical information.

There will also be the records of the proceedings of the local
authority, with accounts of their financial officers, sometimes even
with the vouchers for payments. Records of such transactions as
the granting of licences, benefactions or endowments may be found
as well as details of the general activities of the district, such as
charitable and official functions. Much of this, if not strictly of
genealogical value, may be of interest in extending information
about known members of a family.

Most county record offices now produce leaflets about records
which are of interest to family historians, and there are guides to
their holdings of parish registers, wills and so on (see p.86-8).

## *Specialised Libraries*

If one comes on some particular technical or otherwise specialised
point one should turn for assistance to the library of the appropriate
society. Many government departments have libraries covering
their own field, and these may be found of assistance.

If an ancestor is known to have belonged to a particular
profession, or to have been a beneficiary of a charitable institution,
information may well be found by investigating the archives of
the body concerned, starting with a letter of enquiry to the librarian.

It will soon be found that, apart from the well-known libraries,
there are many others, both in London and elsewhere in the
country, which can be of use to the genealogist. The searcher living
outside the capital should not omit to investigate the possibilities.

CHAPTER 12

# Other sources

In this chapter something will be said of a variety of sources of information, some of which have been mentioned only incidentally in the previous chapters.

## *Manorial Records*

There is a vast quantity of manorial records extant and scattered amongst most important repositories of archives in the country. A register is kept by the National Register of Archives, Quality House, Quality Court, Chancery Lane, London, WC2 1HF. Anybody interested in a particular manor should inquire of the Registrar there for information as to the whereabouts of such records. The Victoria County History (which covers most counties) has a section under each county dealing with manors, and full reference to sources is given in footnotes.

The main items of interest to genealogists are the court rolls, the records of the courts held, usually with the Steward presiding. Important information is given by these, as they include admissions to tenancies on the death of a tenant. Normally the heir was admitted on payment of a fine and his relationship to the deceased is recorded. The Court also had a disciplinary function as is illustrated by the court roll reproduced in plate 9 (p.74), where it will be seen various tenants were 'presented' for not keeping their houses, hedges, etc., in repair.

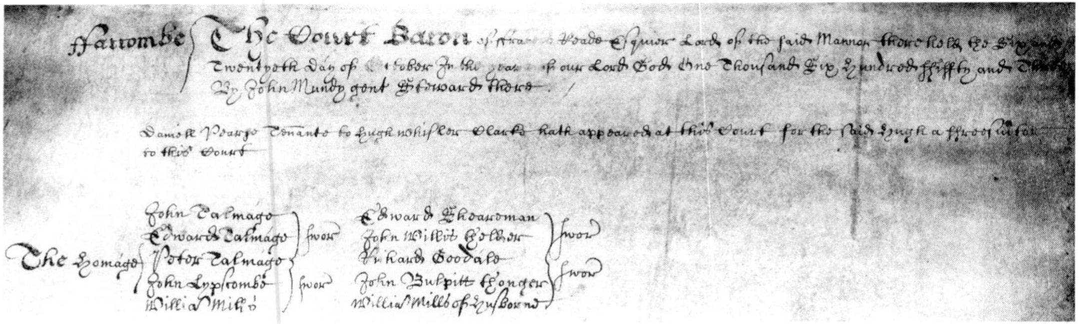

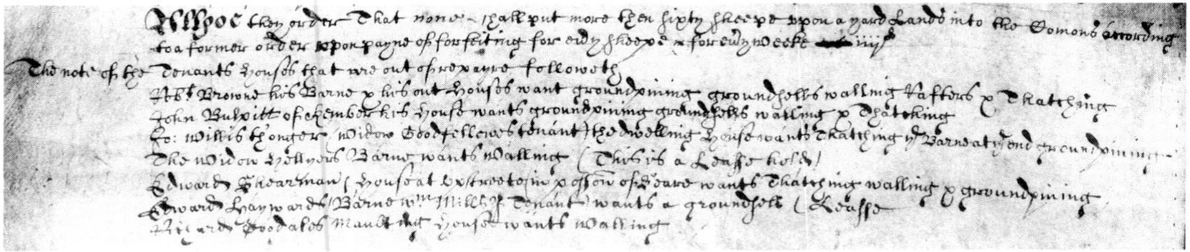

**Plate 9** *A Manorial Court Roll (from the British Library, Add. Charters 5077).*
*(By permission of the British Library.)*

## Newspapers

The British Library's collection of newspapers (except for London papers prior to 1801) is kept at its Newspaper Library, Colindale Avenue, Colindale, London NW7 5HE, but local record offices and libraries often hold collections in their archives. One must remember that in the earlier days of newspapers–the 18th and 19th centuries–facilities for delivery were not what they are today. There was no London paper delivered to the provinces on the day of issue. Local papers, therefore, contained the national as well as the local news, with the result that the latter was often limited to a few paragraphs about each principal town in the district. From quite early issues there are records of births, marriages and deaths, though, again, to a very much smaller extent than today. Local advertisements are sometimes of interest as containing particulars of properties, public announcements etc.

## Periodicals

A number of periodicals survive from the 18th century, such as *The Historical Register* or *The Gentleman's Magazine*, which recorded births, marriages and deaths and the movements of the nobility and gentry. Another periodical, *Notes and Queries*, which still exists today, sometimes refers to genealogical matter. There are usually index volumes to a series of this type of periodical.

There were at one time genealogical periodicals such as *The Ancestor*, *The Genealogist* or *The Pedigree Register*, and the indexes to these may be worth referring to. At the present day the main periodical on the subject is *The Genealogists' Magazine*, issued by the Society of Genealogists. This gives particulars of accessions to the Society's Library and records current matters of interest to the genealogist.

## *Poll Books*

Poll books give a return of those who voted at Parliamentary elections and therefore give a fairly full list of the property owners of the district, the vote being then entirely based on property qualification. They are mostly of late 18th- and early 19th-century date, though a few of earlier date survive in some counties. Inquiry should be made of county archivists who will probably know what copies exist. The collections at the Society of Genealogists and Guildhall Library in London have already been mentioned (pages 64 and 71).

## *Monumental Inscriptions*

This term (abbreviated by the genealogist to M.I.s) covers both gravestones in churchyards or inside churches and memorial tablets not at the place of burial. These sometimes give information as to dates of death, names of husband or wife, children, etc. Where the deceased had recently moved from another place, they sometimes give his former place of residence–or, if erected there, they give the place to which he had moved. The tracing of a family move is one of the constant problems in genealogical research. M.I.s mostly refer to the gentry, so one cannot expect to find memorials to the humbler families in the village church.

Churchyard memorials of the 18th century are often illegible now, though some of good stone in sheltered places can still be deciphered, if carefully examined, and others, the inscriptions of which have been re-cut, are reasonably clear. When the parish of the family is known, the churchyard should be visited with the possibility in view. For the earlier 19th century, before the establishment of the General Register Office, they make a useful supplement to information in the parish register, and even after that date they may amplify a death certificate.

There are records of M.I.s both in print and in manuscript. Inquiry should always be made at the local record office or large reference library, as a copy may have been deposited there. The largest collection in the country is at the Society of Genealogists' Library in London, and there is a list available from the Society, in two sections, Part 1 covering Southern England, and Part 2 covering Northern England, Wales, Scotland and Ireland.

## *Biography*

Many of the public schools have printed registers of their pupils, in some cases going back to the 15th century. The information given varies: sometimes it includes name and occupation of father. The Universities of Oxford and Cambridge have such printed lists, known as 'Alumni Oxonienses' and 'Alumni Cantabrigienses'. Some of the other Universities and each of the Inns of Court have similar lists. Often a brief biographical note will be found in these registers.

For officers in the services, old Navy or Army Lists will be found useful, and there are Clerical and Medical Directories for the clergy and doctors, while other professions (such as solicitors, architects, surveyors and engineers) all have their own professional bodies, whose libraries would be worth consulting. There are even printed biographical works available in larger reference libraries for some of these professions, as well as for painters, sculptors, writers and musicians.

If an ancestor held some official position, such as sheriff, justice of the peace, mayor or alderman, appropriate lists can be seen in the relevant record office or public library.

Of course anyone who achieved fame or notoriety may well appear in the *Dictionary of National Biography* (which runs into many volumes), or *Who Was Who*, which reprints entries from *Who's Who* from 1897 onwards, after the subjects' deaths.

Genealogical information on the peerage and gentry can be found in *Burke's Peerage* and *Burke's Landed Gentry*, but these publications only cover a tiny proportion of the population.

## Guilds and Trade Associations

Since the formation of guilds of merchants in early days there have been trade associations of various kinds. Such bodies as the various Livery Companies of the City of London, each of which relates to a trade, have records of their proceedings, admissions to their register, apprenticeships etc. In the case of anybody in trade or business in or near London the records of the relative Livery Company should be looked up. They may be at Guildhall or still in the custody of the Company.

County or municipal authorities will probably be able to give information through their archivist or librarian of local guilds or associations which existed, and the survival of their records.

## Family Histories and Pedigrees

A number of family histories have been prepared from time to time and these mostly include pedigrees. Some may be unreliable, particularly those which, to cover a gap in the evidence, say 'from whom was descended ...'. It should be fairly easy to see whether each step is properly substantiated. Pedigrees will also be found in manuscript in various libraries and record offices. All these records again refer to the gentry and do not help the humbler families.

If there is any possibility that a right to armorial bearings has been recorded, the College of Arms should be consulted (enquiries should be addressed to the Officer in Waiting, College of Arms, Queen Victoria Street, London EC4V 4BT). Its records are not open to the public but for a fee a search can be made to establish whether any family of a particular name is on record as entitled to a coat of arms.

If a right to arms is to be established it will be necessary to prove direct male descent from one of the families whose arms are in the official records of the College of Arms, and to register the pedigree at the College. Every statement in the pedigree must be supported by legally acceptable evidence from contemporary records, and the pedigree will be carefully scrutinised by two of the officers at the College before being accepted. The officers (the Kings, Heralds and Pursuivants of Arms), though appointed by the Crown, are mainly dependent on the fees paid for the services they render: those who consult them must, therefore, expect to pay on a scale suitable for professional experts.

## *Leases*

Leases may provide useful information about a family and its movements, though they are not often likely to give direct evidence of descent. Such records are now usually deposited in county record offices, who should be consulted about surviving records for a particular locality.

## *Maps*

Old maps are useful in identifying the hundreds or wapentakes (areas of local administration) into which a county was divided; these are needed in searching some early records. A map of the area where a family lived should always be studied (reprints of the first edition of the Ordnance Survey maps are useful here), as the configuration of the ground and directions of roads may provide a clue to movements. One must remember that transport was very restricted, even in the early 19th century, and that a horse, with or without a cart, was the principal means of transport for any distance that could not be walked.

Tithe maps, produced as a result of the Tithe Commutation Act of 1836 (6 & 7 Wm.IV, c.71), are large scale maps giving names of landowners and occupiers with details of their holdings and land cultivation. Copies are at the Public Record Office and in county record offices.

## Sundry Reference Books

Some of the most useful reference books are the various printed indexes to records. The Harleian Society and the British Record Society in particular have each issued a series of volumes including indexes to wills, marriage allegations and copies of parish registers. The catalogue of the British Library or of any library which has a series should be looked at to see whether there are any indexes referring to the county or diocese in which the searcher is interested. There are also officially published indexes to some of the public records.

Another group of books often referred to are books of topography, particularly the older ones which give information about old names of places, administrative boundaries etc., at the time of their publication. It is often useful to know which hundred or wapentake a parish was in. Old histories will be found of each county, and a more modern production, *The Victoria County History*, covers most counties. For many counties the publication is in several volumes and in some cases the series is not yet complete. In the case of London *The Greater London Council Survey of London* may help to fill a gap.

Many counties have or have had archaeological societies which include genealogy among their interests, or even a more specialised parish register society. These societies have usually published their transactions, as well as produced particular volumes on special subjects. There are also efforts of individuals who have written the history of a parish and included a copy of or extracts from the parish registers and other documents, or who have even made a survey of some particular branch of records over a wider field.

A most useful guide to what books are available is *A Genealogist's Bibliography* by C.R. Humphery-Smith (revised edition 1984).

## *Advertisement and Friendship*

Help can sometimes be obtained by advertisements in a suitable periodical. The *Genealogists' Magazine* has a section for Readers' Queries, as well as space for advertisements proper.

I usually look through the Readers' Queries in the *Genealogists' Magazine* in case I can be of help, and one day an unusual name which I knew I had met caught my eye. I had been sorting and listing documents in the Diocesan Registry at Winchester and on looking up my index I found there was a stray will there under that name, deposited with the court in an ecclesiastical cause and never returned. This gave the inquirer two generations which he told me he had been trying to find for ten years.

Genealogists try, too, to help each other, knowing that if they have found something likely to be useful to another, the other searcher may never come across it and it will be lost to him for ever.

In this connection should be mentioned the growth of local Family History Societies and One-name Societies, which enable people of similar interests to meet and exchange information. They are run under the aegis of the Federation of Family History Societies which fosters many genealogical projects, including the ambitious scheme of compiling county marriage indexes as an extension of Boyd's work. Information as to these societies can be obtained from the Administrator, Federation of Family History Societies, c/o Benson Room, Birmingham and Midland Institute, Margaret Street, Birmingham B3 3BS, or from the Guild of One Name Studies, Box G, c/o 14 Charterhouse Buildings, Goswell Road, London EC1M 7BA.

## *Professional Help*

A professional genealogist can either be asked to undertake specific searches, or can be given a wider brief and asked to carry out as much work as possible to trace a particular family within specified financial limits. This can be invaluable to someone no longer living in the same part of the country as their ancestors, as a researcher in the area will have specialist knowledge of local sources and local history, which could, in the long run, save much time and expense.

Those wishing to consult a professional genealogist are advised to consult the list published by the Association of Genealogists and Record Agents (A.G.R.A.), which gives the names, addresses and special interests of members all over the country. Copies may be seen in most record offices and libraries, or may be obtained from the Hon. Secretary, 1 Woodside Close, Stanstead Road, Caterham, Surrey CR3 6AU, or the Society of Genealogists.

CHAPTER 13

# Conclusion

There is no conclusion to genealogy; even if one line of descent comes to an apparent dead end, there are others to be pursued. The scope is infinite, as searches can be made for the ancestry of all four grandparents, then their parents, and so on, almost *ad infinitum*.

Even the most hopeless case should never be completely abandoned, as some hitherto unknown records may come to light, or information from an unexpected source may turn up, perhaps quite by chance, and this can be the long-awaited breakthrough.

Another approach, when a family tree has been traced back for two or three hundred years, is to try to flesh out the bare bones of the line of descent, using some of the other local records mentioned in Chapters 6, 8, 11 and 12, as described by Arthur Willis (see pp.118-123).

It should be fairly straightforward to trace a pedigree back to the early 1800s (although even this has been known to cause problems), but before the 19th century there are many obstacles, such as the removal of a family from one place to another or a gap in the records. At this date so many official sources are lacking that almost anything *might* provide a clue; skill lies in seeing the possibilities, weighing them, picking out the probabilities with some idea of their relative likelihood, and testing them systematically and thoroughly.

The main problems for most of those who want to trace their family trees are distance from the sources to be investigated and/ or lack of time. These can be met to a certain extent by carrying out the research by correspondence, but naturally this is less satisfactory than direct searching.

Sometimes a half-and-half method may be used: to pursue the subject oneself where practicable, but employing a local searcher for particular tasks, such as examining a certain parish register for a given period, or making abstracts of a number of possible wills. There is, of course, the alternative of handing over the whole problem to a professional, but this has the disadvantage that one is less in touch with the actual research, so missing the excitement of the chase and, not least, the cost is apt to mount up.

Speaking of cost, it must be emphasised that there is absolutely no fixed relation between expenditure and results. A whole day may be spent in seeing a parish register and the search prove to be in vain–it may even be that a hoped-for entry is not there because there is a gap of a few years at the vital date, due to the forgetfulness of an 18th-century parson or parish clerk. It is, therefore, quite impossible to answer a question such as 'How much will it cost to trace my family tree?'.

As stated on p.1 of this book, do remember to take the search back a step at a time, not leaping ahead to conclusions which may later prove to be wrong. It is much more satisfying to be sure of the links between one generation and the next than to produce an impressively long but tentative pedigree, riddled with question marks and dotted lines.

Finally, have fun, and enjoy the feeling of achievement as your knowledge of your ancestors increases.

# A Bibliography for Beginners

O ut of the many books on the subject the following selection has been made with the beginner in mind. Those in print are obtainable by post or to personal callers from the Phillimore Bookshop, Shopwyke Manor Barn, Chichester, West Sussex PO20 6BG. A catalogue will be sent free on request.

## General Guides

G. Hamilton-Edwards, *In Search of Ancestry* (revised edn., 1983)
G. Pelling, *Beginning Your Family History* (1995)
D. Hey, *The Oxford Guide to Family History* (1993)
A.J. Camp, *Everyone has Roots* (1978)
A.J. Camp, *First Steps in Family History* (1996)

## Recording Searches

Society of Genealogists Leaflets: *Family Records and their Layout* (1994), *Note Taking and Keeping for Genealogists* (1994), *Computers in Genealogy Beginners Hand Book* (1994)
I. Swinnerton, *Basic Approach to Keeping your Family Records* (1995)
D. Hawgood, *Computers for Family History: An Introduction* (4th edn., 1992) and *Genealogy Computer Packages* (1994)
*Handling and Preserving Family Records*, a Video guide, available from Cable Crouch Productions Ltd., Greatness Lane, Sevenoaks, Kent TN14 5BQ
Lynskey, Marie, *Family Trees, A Manual for their Design, Layout and Display* (1996)

## Interpretation

M. Gandy, *Basic Approach to Latin for Family Historians* (1995)

E.A. Gooder, *Latin for Local History* (7th impression, 1990)

H.E.P. Grieve, *Examples of English Handwriting 1150-1750* (5th impression 1981)

F.G. Emmison, *How to Read Local Archives 1550-1700* (1988)

C.T. Martin, *The Record Interpreter* (reprinted 1994)

J. Morris, *A Latin Glossary for Family and Local Historians* (reprinted 1995)

D. Stuart, *Latin for Local and Family Historians* (1995)

E.E. Thoyts, *How to Read Old Documents* (reprinted 1980)

C.R. Cheney, *Handbook of Dates for Students of English History* (1970)

L. Munby, *Reading Tudor and Stuart Handwriting* (1988)

## Census Returns

J.S.W. Gibson & C. Chapman, *Census Indexes and Indexing* (1988)

J.S.W. Gibson, *Census Returns on Microfilm: a Directory to Local Holdings* (6th edn., 1994)

## Parish Registers

C.R. Humphery-Smith (ed.), *The Phillimore Atlas and Index of Parish Registers* (2nd ed., 1995)

*National Index of Parish Registers* (1968- ): Vol. 1, *Sources of Births, Marriages and Deaths before 1837*, Vol. 2, *Sources of Nonconformist Genealogy and Family History*, Vol. 3, *Sources for Roman Catholic and Jewish Genealogy and Family History*, and subsequent volumes for many individual counties.

*Parish Registers Copies in the Library of the Society of Genealogists* (11th edn., 1995)

*A List of Parishes in Boyd's Marriage Index* (6th edn., 1987, reprinted 1994)

E. McLaughlin, *Making the most of the I.G.I.* (updated 1995)

J.S.W. Gibson, *Bishop's Transcripts and Marriage Licences, Bonds and Allegations: A Guide to their Location and Indexes* (3rd edn., 1991)

M. Gandy (ed.), *Catholic Parishes in England, Wales and Scotland, an Atlas* (1993)

Society of Genealogists Booklets in the series *My Ancestors Were ... on Baptists, Congregationalists in England and Wales, English Presbyterians/Unitarians, Jewish, Methodists, Quakers*

W.G. Tate, *The Parish Chest* (reprinted 1983)

## Wills

J.S.W. Gibson, *Probate Jurisdictions: Where to Look for Wills* (4th edn., 1994)

## Public Record Office

J. Cox & T. Padfield, *Tracing Your Ancestors in the Public Record Office* revised by A. Bevan & A. Duncan (4th edn. 1990)

J. Cox, *Never Been Here Before?* (P.R.O. Readers' Guide No.4, 1993)

P.R.O. Information Leaflets and Family Fact Sheets on all classes of records of interest to genealogists

J.S.W. Gibson, M. Medlycott & D. Mills, *Land and Window Tax Assessments* (1993)

N.A.M. Rodger, *Naval Records for Genealogists* (P.R.O. 1988)

## Society of Genealogists' Library

*Using the Library of the Society of Genealogists* (1996)

Lists and Indexes to the Society's holdings of Directories and Poll Books, Parish Register Copies, Monumental Inscriptions and other sources are all available from the Society

## Other Libraries and Record Offices

J.W. Moulton, *Genealogical Resources in English Repositories* (1988 and Supplement, 1992)

*Record Repositories in Great Britain* (9th edn., 3rd impression 1994)

R. Harvey, *A Guide to Genealogical Sources in the Guildhall Library* (3rd edn., 1988)

J.S.W. Gibson, *Quarter Sessions Records for Family Historians: A Select List* (4th edn. 1995)

J. Gibson & P. Peskett, *Record Offices: How to find them* (1996)


## Other Sources

D. Stuart, *Manorial Records* (1992)

C.R. Chapman, *An Introduction to using Newspapers and Periodicals* (1993)

S. Bourne & A.H. Chicken, *Records of the Medical Profession* (1994)

W. Foot, *Maps for Family History* (1994)

*Register of One-Name Studies* (11th edn., 1995)

*The Association of Genealogists and Record Agents: List of Members* (regularly updated, obtainable from the Society of Genealogists)

C.R. Humphery-Smith, *A Genealogist's Bibliography* (1984)

G.W. Marshall, *The Genealogist's Guide* (1973)

J.W. Whitmore, *A Genealogical Guide* (1953)

G.B. Barrow, *The Genealogist's Guide* (1977)


## Wales, Scotland and Ireland

J. Rowlands & others (ed.), *Welsh Family History: A Guide to Research* (1993)

G.K. Hamilton-Edwards, *In Search of Scottish Ancestry* (reprinted 1983)

C. Sinclair, *Tracing Your Scottish Ancestors: A Guide to Ancestry Research in the Scottish Record Office* (4th impression 1995)

J. Grenham, *Tracing Your Irish Ancestors* (1992)

S. Helferty & R. Refausse, *Directory of Irish Archives* (2nd edn., 1993)

# Regnal Years

Dates in older manuscripts are often expressed by the regnal year. To be quite sure which year is referred to it is necessary to know the day of the year in which the reign officially began. For instance, the reign of Queen Elizabeth I began on 17 November 1558. From 17 November 1558 to 16 November 1559 was therefore the year 1 Eliz. The year 3 Eliz. would begin two years later, i.e. 17 November 1560. The year 34 Eliz. would being 33 years later, i.e. on 17 November 1591.

There are in some cases short gaps between the official dates at the beginning of a new reign, but, apart from these and a complication in the reign of John (in the case of John, regnal years are calculated from Ascension Day each year, which is a moveable feast in the calendar. For full details see *The Oxford Companion to English Literature*, Appendix IV), a simple calculation from the opening dates given below will enable a date expressed by regnal year to be identified.

Dates are not given here after the reign of Queen Victoria, as the regnal year is then practically only used for Acts of Parliament and in their case is expressed differently, as it must be related to the Parliamentary Session in which the Act is passed.

| | |
|---|---|
| William I | 25 Dec. 1066 |
| William II | 26 Sept. 1087 |
| Henry I | 5 Aug. 1100 |
| Stephen | 26 Dec. 1135 |
| Henry II | 19 Dec. 1154 |
| Richard I | 3 Sept. 1189 |
| John* | 27 May 1199 |
| Henry III | 28 Oct. 1216 |
| Edward I | 20 Nov. 1272 |
| Edward II | 8 July 1307 |
| Edward III | 25 Jan. 1327 |
| Richard II | 22 June 1377 |
| Henry IV | 30 Sept. 1399 |
| Henry V | 21 Mar. 1413 |
| Henry VI | 1 Sept. 1422 |
| Edward IV | 4 Mar. 1461 |
| Edward V | 9 Apr. 1483 |
| Richard III | 26 June 1483 |
| Henry VII | 22 Aug. 1485 |
| Edward VI | 28 Jan. 1547 |
| Mary | 6 July 1553 |
| Philip and Mary | 25 July 1554 |
| Elizabeth I | 17 Nov. 1558 |
| James I | 24 Mar. 1603 |
| Charles I | 27 Mar. 1625 |

\* in the case of John, regnal years are calculated from Ascension Day each year, which is a moveable feast in the calendar. For full details see *The Oxford Companion to English Literature*, Appendix IV

† No regnal year was used during the Commonwealth 30 Jan. 1649 to 29 May 1660. On the Restoration the years of the reign of Charles II were dated from the death of Charles I on the principle that he had been King *de jure* since then

Commonwealth†
Charles II                          30 Jan. 1649
James II                            6 Feb. 1685
(Interregnum 12 Dec. 1688 to 12 Feb. 1689)
William III and Mary                13 Feb. 1689
William III                         28 Dec. 1694
Anne                                8 Mar. 1702
George I                            1 Aug. 1714
George II                           11 June 1727
George III                          25 Oct. 1760
George IV                           29 Jan. 1820
William IV                          26 June 1830
Victoria                            20 June 1837

The reader might like to be reminded here of the change in the method of dating which came into force in 1752 (see p.22).

It is also useful to know that early documents were dated by reference to the nearest festival of the church. *A Handbook of Dates* by C.R. Cheney gives all the saints' days and festivals. It also sets out all the regnal years with numbers referring to tables which provided calendars for each year.

# Foot of a Fine

Note: The bold type and italics are the author's in an attempt to make the reading easier.

This is the final concord made in the Court of the Lady Queen at Westminster on the octave of the Purification of Blessed Mary (*Feb. 9*) in the eighth year of the reign of Anne (*1710*) by God's grace queen of Great Britain, France and Ireland, Defender of the Faith, etc. after the Conquest, in the presence of Thomas Trevor, John Blencoe, Robert Tracy and Robert Dormer, justices and other faithful subjects of the Lady Queen then present there, **between** *David Clarke, John Lampard, John Broadwood* and *James Mitchell,* plaintiffs **and** *Elizabeth* his wife, *Robert Crosse, Joan Broadway,* widow, and *William Mumford* and *Brigit* his wife, deforciants; **concerning** four messuages and three gardens with appurtenances in the City of Winchester, **whence a plea of agreement** was summoned between them in the same court, namely that the aforesaid James Crosse & Elizabeth, Robert, Joan & Brigit recognise that the aforesaid tenements with appurtenances are the right of David, as those which the same David, John, John and James Mitchell have by gift of the aforesaid James Crosse & Elizabeth, Joan & William & Brigit & their heirs to the aforesaid David, John, John & James Mitchell & the heirs of David for ever. **And furthermore** the same *James Crosse* & *Elizabeth* granted for themselves and the heirs of that James that they guarantee to the aforesaid David, John, John, & James Mitchell & David's heirs the aforesaid tenements with appurtenances against the aforesaid James Crosse and Elizabeth and James' heirs for ever. **And further** the same *Robert* granted for himself and his heirs that they guarantee to the aforesaid

David, John, John and James Mitchell & David's heirs the aforesaid tenements with appurtenances against the aforesaid Robert and his heirs for ever. **And in addition** the same *Joan* granted for herself and her heirs that they guarantee to the aforesaid David, John, John and James Mitchell & David's heirs the aforesaid tenements with appurtenances against the aforesaid Joan and her heirs for ever. **And also** the same *William* & *Brigit* granted for themselves and William's heirs that they guarantee to the aforesaid David, John, John & James Mitchell & David's heirs the aforesaid tenements with appurtenances against the aforesaid William & Brigit and William's heirs for ever. **And for this** recognition, remission, quit-claim, guarantee, fine & concord the said David, John, John & James Mitchell gave the aforesaid James Crosse & Elizabeth, Robert, Joan & William *two hundred pounds sterling*.

Public Record Office Ref. CP 25 (2)/964, 8 Anne, Hilary.

Translated from the Latin by the College of Arms.

# Some Problems Solved

(Note: the surnames in this chapter are fictitious, but the incidents are based on fact.)

## 1. Jane Pink

### Question of identity solved by a gravestone

Jane Pink was married in 1792 at Colchester to Henry Brown; they were Wesleyans throughout their married life. Judging from her age at death, Jane was born about 1771/2, and searches were made for her parentage, but no baptism in this name was found in any Anglican parish in Colchester. From the records of the town's Wesleyan Chapel, it was known that a William Pink was a member there in the later 18th century, but the chapel's baptism register begins only in 1793, too late for Jane's baptism, or for any children of William Pink.

However there was a Jane Pink, daughter of William and Mary Pink, baptised in 1772 at the Lion Walk Independent Chapel in Colchester. There was also a Jane Pink of Colchester married in 1799 to Francis White. Which Jane was which?

Of course it seemed likely that the Jane Pink married in 1792 was the daughter of the Wesleyan William Pink, since she was a Wesleyan for the whole of her adult life, but extensive research was undertaken in various classes of Colchester records, and in Essex probate records in an effort to find further evidence–all entirely without success.

Eventually, printed histories of the Wesleyan Chapel and the Lion Walk Chapel in Colchester were examined. The account of the Lion Walk Independent Chapel includes copies of inscriptions on the monuments in the burial ground. The last two in the list refer to William Pink and his wife Mary, and Francis White and his wife Jane. This made it clear that Jane Pink of the Independent Chapel, baptised in 1772, was the same person as Jane Pink married in 1799, buried many years later beside her parents and her husband. The Jane Pink who married Henry Brown in 1792, would therefore have been the daughter of the Wesleyan William Pink.

As the two Janes had the same unusual surname, and their fathers also bore the same Christian name, they could well have been related to one another, but that is another story!

## 2. James West
### Value of an Unusual Christian Name

James West, tavern house-keeper in Westminster, died in 1794 leaving a large family. His will disclosed, *inter alia*, that he had two brothers, Michael and Marmaduke, both farmers, the former in Buckinghamshire and the latter in Surrey. The natural inference that the family came from one of these areas proved to be without foundation. Marmaduke is not a common name, and as it was used in several subsequent generations it was suspected of being an ancestral name, perhaps for many generations. It was known to be a very popular name in Yorkshire. The calendars of wills proved at York were therefore consulted with the result that two of that name were found, one testator mentioning in his will sons named Michael, James and Marmaduke. An examination of the registers of this testator's parish gave all necessary particulars, including the marriages of two of the brothers: moreover, the actual date of baptism of the other was found to agree with that mentioned in the family papers of his branch of the family.

## 3. Edward White

### Family Surnames Given as Christian Names

Edward White died in 1825, aged 60, in a village on the borders of Oxfordshire and Berkshire, his origin being unknown. He was Lord of the Manor and had considerable property in the neighbourhood. A history of the parish, long out of print but subsequently located (being privately printed it was not in the B.L.), showed that the surname of the previous Lords of the Manor was Francis. As Edward White had given several of his children Francis as one of their Christian names, a relationship was suspected.

He also gave his children as Christian names other names which were evidently surnames–Hayward, Vince and Gatacre. On the wills of the Francis family being found and examined it was noticed that this family was related to Haywards, Vinces and Gatacres, farmers. One will showed that a member of the Francis family lived at a town in Northamptonshire, and in the parish registers there references were found to all these three families as far back as 1680. The marriage entry of a White in 1760 in that parish described him as of another nearby town; this took the search there and gave the ancestry to Edward White. His relationship to the Francis family was found to be through the Haywards four generations earlier.

## 4. Thomas Mason

### Unusual value from the records of a City Livery Company

Thomas Mason, whose ancestry was being sought, was known to have been a freeman of one of the City Livery Companies of London in the middle of the 19th century. Enquiry of the Company showed that he had been apprenticed to his grandfather, also a freeman of the same Company. A search of the books showed that two uncles, two cousins, two great-uncles and his great-grandfather had all been freemen too. In the record of the great-grandfather's apprenticeship was the name of his father. Though one might expect some information about a known member of a Company and, perhaps, the name of his father, it was a surprise to find such a complete pedigree available.

## 5. Joseph Yeoman

### Flaw in an apparently perfect pedigree

The ancestry of Joseph Yeoman had been traced back through eight generations to an Essex farmer, George Yeoman, with what seemed to be an undoubtedly correct pedigree.

However, during a search in a neighbouring parish for details of another branch of the family, a fault in the pedigree was found, quite by chance. A Thomas Yeoman, third from George in the direct line of the 'proved' pedigree, who had been named in his father's will to succeed to the family farm, had, in fact, died between the dates of his father's will and death, was buried in the neighbouring parish and could not, therefore, have succeeded. It was, however, known that a Thomas Yeoman did in fact succeed to the farm on the testator's death.

Following a long search it was found that the second Thomas was a distant cousin, who had succeeded not so much by virtue of kinship but because he had married a female descendant of an earlier generation, heiress on failure of the male line. It was from this second Thomas that Joseph was descended: George Yeoman was in fact a great-uncle of the second Thomas.

## 6. Flora Lambert (?Hutchins)
### A Mistake in a Census Record

A census return gave a family listed thus with ages and places of birth:

| | |
|---|---|
| John Lambert | Head |
| Mary Lambert | wife |
| Mary Lambert | U daughter |
| Robert Lambert | U son |
| Elizabeth Hutchins | M daughter |
| Mary Lambert | granddaughter |
| Flora Lambert | granddaughter |

The two granddaughters are apparently daughters of a son of John Lambert, but there was no such son known of in the pedigree and hardly room for a place for him between his known brother and sisters. Suspicion was at once aroused that a mistake had been made and that Mary and Flora (both under seven years of age) were children of Elizabeth Hutchins. To solve the problem a birth certificate was searched for, Flora being chosen as having the less common name and both surnames Lambert and Hutchins being looked for in the index. Age and place being known, an entry of Flora Hutchins was easily found and on the full certificate being received it was seen that she was the daughter of Elizabeth Hutchins (*née* Lambert). The enumerator must have slipped in entering the surnames. This emphasises that even a written record must not be regarded as infallible.

## 7. Charlotte Anne's Marriage
### The Value of Army Records

Charlotte Anne Browne was known to have married the following:
(1) in 1852 Charles Henry Osborne, who died 1854

(2) date unknown, Richard James Wright, died 1859

(3) in 1860, John Whitbread.

The problem was to find the record of her marriage to Richard James Wright. A search of the marriage indexes at St Catherine's House revealed the marriage of a Richard James Wright in the December Quarter 1856, but Charlotte Anne Osborne did not appear in the index for the same quarter. However,. the certificate was obtained, and proved to be the marriage of Richard James Wright to Charlotte Anne Maclean. No record of this marriage could be found, neither could any will be found for Maclean. However, as Charlotte Anne's husband Whitbread was a captain serving in India at the time of his marriage, a search was made of the *Army Lists* for the relevant period, and an Andrew Scott Maclean was found, also serving in India. A search of *Widow's Pensions Applications* (WO 42) at the P.R.O. at Kew revealed that Charlotte Anne Osborne had married Andrew Scott Maclean in August 1854 in Ceylon, and that he had died in Bombay a month later.

## 8. Samuel Vachell Hicks
### A Problem of Age

The 1875 marriage certificate of Samuel Vachell Hicks, bachelor, gave his age as 'of full age'. On the assumption that this implied over 21, a search of ten years was made for a birth certificate for him, but none was found. A subsequent search of his bride's address in the 1871 Census Returns revealed Samuel Vachell Hicks living there as a 'lodger', his age being given as 48, and his place of birth a parish in Devon. A search was then made of the relevant parish register, backwards and forwards from 1823, and his baptism was eventually found in 1817 (the unusual name confirmed that it was the right entry). But for the fact that he was living with his future father-in-law in 1871, it would have been very difficult to trace him. One might perhaps assume that he did not want his bride (who was 25 years younger) to know his real age, since when he married he was, in fact, 58!

## 9. Benjamin Palmer
### Unusual Revelation of Illegitimacy

Benjamin Palmer, son of Henry Palmer and Sarah, née Hill, was believed to have been born in a parish in Oxfordshire in 1844, but no birth certificate could be found for him in that year. The 1851 Census Returns showed the household of Henry Palmer and his wife Sarah, and, living with them a child, Benjamin Palmer Hill, aged 6, 'son, illegitimate'. Another search was then made for the birth certificate for the date alleged, and he was found as the son of Sarah Hill. The marriage certificate of Henry Palmer and Sarah Hill showed that they were married five months after the birth of Benjamin.

## 10. George Myring
### A vital clue from the I.G.I.

George Myring and his wife Phoebe had six children baptised at Stoke Damerel, Devon, between 1760 and 1770. This was the parish for Devonport, where George worked as a ropemaker. However, no trace of him could be found before 1760, despite searches in local parish registers and in the International Genealogical Index (I.G.I.) for Devon and adjacent counties.

Through the Society of Genealogists, contact was made with others working on the same name, one of whom happened to mention in a letter, 'Although you are probably aware of the following I thought I should mention it ...' He went on to say that nationwide searches in the I.G.I. for all Myring entries had produced the marriage of George Myring and Phebe [sic] Brill in

Portsea in 1756, and the baptism of their son John in 1757, but no further entries for this couple in Hampshire. He continued, 'We had assumed that, because of the dockyard connection, they moved to Stoke Damerel', where their later children were baptised.

In fact George Myring's descendants were *not* aware of this information and, with the combination of the dockyard connection, an unusual surname and the wife's unusual Christian name, it proved to be the long-awaited breakthrough.

# A Genealogical Adventure

*by*

Arthur J. Willis

# Introduction

This section is a shortened version of Arthur Willis' *A Genealogical Adventure*, which formed the last 10 chapters of previous editions of this book. Although his initial efforts appear somewhat misdirected, and should not be imitated by amateur genealogists of today, due allowance must be made for the ignorance of the author. When he embarked on his 'Adventure', in the early 1950s, Arthur Willis could find no text book later than *How to write the History of a Family* (Phillimore, 1887) and its *Supplement* (1900), he did not know of the Society of Genealogists, and only at a late stage realised that there was such a thing as a county record office! Consequently he had to proceed by trial and error, discovering seemingly obvious sources only as he became better acquainted with the subject. Readers will also notice that there have been changes in the location of records and even of names (e.g. The British Library), but these have not been altered here.

In one respect Arthur Willis was more fortunate than those embarking on such a quest today–having been born in 1895, he was able to glean enough information from older members of the family and from various family papers to take the pedigree straight back to the early 19th century, thus by-passing the usual routine of birth and marriage certificates, and census returns, which are the unavoidable lot of younger genealogists. This should be borne in mind when reading his account, as there are few nowadays lucky enough to have such a head start.

However, the author's infectious enthusiasm and curiosity about his ancestors, and his dogged persistence and boundless optimism, even when faced with insuperable obstacles, make this a fascinating and inspiring account of one man's search for his family's roots. It also gives a very real taste of the thrill of the genealogical chase, of the triumphs and the frustrations that may be encountered, and I hope that others, while benefiting from the huge advances made in this field over the past 50 years, will experience for themselves the same delight in their discoveries.

K.E.P.

# Archives and Heirlooms

The story opens with a boy of nine, sent home to boarding school by parents living abroad and spending a good deal of his holidays in the house of his grandfather in Ealing. Over the mantelpiece in the dining room hung a low-relief portrait of an elderly gentleman modelled in red wax and enclosed in a red plush mount and heavy rococo frame, with several miniatures below it. Despite a lack of precise information, it was vaguely understood that these were ancestors who had lived in Winchester, where the family was in some sort of trade.

Not long after this my grandfather died. The house remained in the occupation of the family until some 40 years later when it was emptied and sold. The pictures mentioned above were passed to me, with the family papers and other oddments. An examination of what I received I found interesting. There were a few wills with original probates and copies of others, a variety of small scraps of paper with genealogical notes and a record of gravestone inscriptions in Winchester, two seals and a notepaper die. The documents included two in legal Latin, a small devotional book and last, but by no means least, the Family Bible.

Enquiry of my father elicited very little about the family history. He had no knowledge of where the family had lived before they came to Winchester, only a vague idea that they were from Hertfordshire. He added that the crest was that of the Hertfordshire family and that the family motto was *Non nobis, Domine.*

My first thought was to put the material received into orderly form and record the information available in a family tree (see pp.127-134).

I had some personal knowledge of my grandfather, James of Ealing, and his two sisters, Sarah and Emma, which I supplemented by enquiry from other family members and the family Bible (plate 1, p.xvi). The next step was to examine the wills to see what earlier generations could be established from them. The backbone of any family tree will be the male line, and there were two male Willis wills, those of James (died 1858), whom I will call James of Winchester, and John (died 1820). I had not received my grandfather's will with the papers, but a visit to Somerset House soon produced it, and I ordered a photostat copy.

I first examined the will of James of Winchester, which was dated in 1854: he described himself as a painter, the first piece of new information. He mentioned his son Henry John and daughters Emma Bown and Maria, and Henry John's three children. From these details I was able to make an outline pedigree back to James.

The next will was that of John (died 1820), who mentioned his wife Mary, son James and daughter Ann Skeate, and James's three children. This added another generation to the direct line.

Other papers included notes of gravestones in Cathedral Yard, Winchester, written by my grandfather, which named the wives of John and James and John's son John, who died aged 13, and several dates. Particularly useful was the information that John (died 1820) was aged 67, thus providing an approximate date of birth.

The other papers included wills of the Skeate family, a newspaper cutting about the marriage of Anne Willis and Ralph Skeate of Sarum in 1809, the wills of Mary Willis (second wife of John), Emma Bown Willis and Mary Gover (1845), a note that one John Willis was a freeman of Winchester in 1730, and an early 18th-century document in Latin relating to property in Winchester and sketches of various Willis coats of arms. These arms apparently belonged to Willis of Fen Ditton, Cambridgeshire and Horingsley and Bales, Hertfordshire (neither of which I could trace in any gazetteer).

# The Search Begins

Having obtained a reader's ticket for the British Museum Reading Room, I went on a visit of exploration. I said I was interested in genealogy and was referred to several genealogical manuals in an open bookcase, and recommended to look up the name 'Phillimore' in the General Catalogue, as he wrote a lot on genealogy.

Among the manuals I found Marshall's *Genealogist's Guide* and under the name of Willis I found references to Berry's *Hampshire Genealogies* and Clutterbuck's *History of Hertfordshire*, which seemed the most likely.

The reference to Clutterbuck's *Hertfordshire* proved to be a pedigree of the Hertfordshire family of Willis, which gave the family of a Richard Willis of Balls Park, two of whose sons were created baronets by Charles I, both titles later becoming extinct. Of more interest to me was the information that Richard had a brother Thomas of Ashe, Hampshire, a village only some 15 miles from Winchester. Might he have had descendants who later moved to Winchester?

The reference to Berry's *Hampshire Genealogies* was to a family of Stoneham Park, which, so far as I knew, had no connection with ours.

I also, as advised, looked up the name of Phillimore and found that he had published a number of volumes of copies of parish registers, including 14 for Hampshire. I first looked through the Winchester parishes for any Willis entries, and found that these were almost all for marriages; of interest was the marriage in 1743 of John Willis to Mary Rumney at St Maurice. It seemed possible that they were the parents of my ancestor John, who was born in

about 1753. As there were no printed copies of the baptism
registers, I realised that a search of the originals must be the next
step.

On a visit to Winchester, I arranged to see the registers of St
Maurice, and searched first for baptisms after 1743, the date of the
marriage. I found the baptisms of a succession of daughters
followed by that of a son John in 1753. This confirmed that John
Willis and Mary Rumney were the parents of John Willis who
died in 1820 aged 67.

I also looked for the burials of the father and mother, and
found a Mary Willis buried in 1758 and John in 1783; as some of
the children were baptised after 1758 it looked as if John had
married again, to another Mary (a very common name at the time),
although there was no burial for her.

A search backwards in the St Maurice registers showed no
earlier Willises, nor could I find any in the neighbouring parish of
St Thomas, so I was still left with the problem of where the first
John Willis was born, and when.

As I had little idea of where to turn and little time to spare for
genealogy, I thought it best to get professional advice and help. I
agreed to more extensive searches being made in Winchester
parish registers for John's baptism, as well as the examination of
other sources, such as wills and apprentice records.

Meanwhile, I made a return visit to the British Museum, and
went through all 14 volumes of Phillimore's *Parish Registers* for
Hampshire, noting all Willis entries, mostly 17th- and 18th-century
marriages. I also came across the Harleian Society publications,
which included two volumes of *Allegations for Marriage Licences
granted by the Bishop of Winchester* (see p.45). Included in these
volumes were licences for John Willis of Hursley in 1718, John of
Hyde Street, Winchester in 1711, Richard of Winchester in 1710,
and another (Christian name not given) at Andover in 1716. These
were all about the date to suit the father of John who married in
1743, but of course not all marriages were by licences. However, I

asked my adviser to add Hursley to the list of parishes he was searching.

I visited Andover myself and found the family of Richard Willis, apothecary, who was married there in 1716 (this was the second marriage for Richard, who was the one married in Winchester in 1710). He had several sons, including a John in 1722; he would have been 21 in 1743, so might have been the one married in that year, and there was a family connection with Winchester.

In due course I received a report from the genealogist. The search of all the Winchester parish registers from 1700 to 1725 produced no baptism which might have been that of John who married in 1743, although there were Willis families in two of the parishes searched.

The registers of Hursley and Stockbridge (and the neighbouring King's Somborne) were also searched, the latter because my father had a vague idea that the family had once settled there before moving to Winchester. In neither case was there any mention of the name during the relevant period.

A search was made for the will of John Willis who died in 1783, which would be of interest even if it did not help with the earlier generations, but none could be found at Winchester or in the P.C.C. indexes. A list was also made of all Willis wills at Winchester from the Civil War to 1800, and one or two which seemed to have some bearing were examined, but neither proved to be of any use. Lists of wills at Salisbury were also searched, in case the family lived just over the county boundary in Wiltshire, but, yet again, nothing likely was found.

The indexes to apprenticeship records had also been searched, but only three Hampshire entries for the surname were found in the 18th century:

1715    John son of John Willis of East Woodhay to William
        Lawrence of the same, pipemaker
1735    James son of John Willis of Kingswood to John

   Willis of the same, attorney
1742  John son of John Willis to Henry Matthew, farrier
   of Henley

These were disappointing as not showing any connection with a family in Winchester, although I noticed that Henley was not far from Ashe, where Thomas of the Cambridgeshire family had lived in the 17th century.

By now the costs of the professional investigation were mounting up but I was myself beginning to get some idea of the possible lines to follow and my interest in the search was deepening, so I decided I would carry on by myself in such time as I had to spare. I need not hurry, and if I found I could do nothing, I could always return to professional help.

As it happened, good luck was waiting only just round the corner.

# A Breakthrough

I thought that the first thing to be done was to spread the net a little wider in searching the Winchester parish registers, so I went back to 1650 in every parish and extracted all the Willis entries, whether relevant or not. I also searched all burials up to 1775, for a possible father of John (married 1743).

This extended search produced the evidence I had seen seeking for so long: in the church St Maurice there were other parish records, as well as registers, stored in the vestry, and among them was a book of settlement certificates (see p.27). One of these related to John Willis, his wife Mary and two children (see plate 6, p.26), and showed that their parish of settlement was East Woodhay (in the north of Hampshire, near the Berkshire border). In view of the names of the children mentioned, there could be no doubt as to identity. Since, in fact, John was not sent back to East Woodhay, he evidently kept his head above water and did not become a charge on the parish.

'East Woodhay' rang a bell–three bells, in fact. There was a record of John Willis of East Woodhay being apprenticed to a pipemaker in 1715 (see p.111), and from the *Hampshire Marriage Licence Allegations* I had noted John Willis, pipemaker, marrying Mary Marchant, at St Thomas, Winchester, in 1718, both described as of Hursley. Thirdly, I recalled that in Phillimore's printed registers I had found a marriage at East Woodhay in 1677 of John Wilis [*sic*] of Faccombe to Susannah White. It looked as though the apprenticeship and the 1718 marriage might refer to the same man, although John must either have been older than usual when apprenticed or was married very young. However, Hursley is about three miles south-west of Winchester, and some 22 miles south of

East Woodhay, so, if it was the same John, it is puzzling that he was apparently living there at the time of his marriage.

Since the parish registers of Hursley had already been searched, without success, for Willis entries, the next step was obviously to look at the registers for East Woodhay. I had them searched for the period 1650-1750 (with burials up to 1780), but my hopes of finding at least one generation of the family recorded there were dashed: apart from one Willes in 1660 and the 1677 marriage of John and Susannah, there was no mention of the name.

My thoughts then turned to adjacent parishes, as John may have been baptised elsewhere, although described as being of East Woodhay at his apprenticeship. I found that the registers of Ashmansworth had been destroyed by fire in 1810, and those of Crux Easton did not begin until 1737 (with some baptisms from 1702), However, registers for the period were extant at Highclere and some of the villages to the north and west of East Woodhay, and at Faccombe, to the south, where I had already noted a Willis entry in the printed copy of the registers.

In due course I had searches made in the years 1650-1750 in the parish registers of Highclere, Combe, Linkenholt, Faccombe, Tangley, Hurstbourne Tarrant and Vernham Dean (all in Hampshire) and West Woodhay, Inkpen, Kintbury, Enborne and Hamstead Marshall (all in Berkshire). Apart from the burial of a John Willis at Hamstead Marshall in December 1715, the only Willis entries were at Faccombe. The registers there were searched back to the beginning in 1585, and produced five generations of the Willis family, ending with John Willis, baptised in 1678, and his brothers and sisters, who were the offspring of the 1677 marriage referred to above.

The registers, unfortunately, confirmed the gap from 1692-1700 which I had already noted in the records of marriages, so there was no sign of the marriage of John who was baptised in 1678. The baptism registers did not include any Willis entries for the years around 1700, when the John who was apprenticed in

1715 would have been born. Though there is no apparent break in the record of baptisms at Faccombe, it sometimes happened that entries were omitted, through error or forgetfulness, but one cannot claim an omission of that sort, failing evidence from some other source. In this case it seems most likely that the elder John was married at Faccombe, Ashmansworth or Crux Easton, and that the younger John was baptised at one of the last two.

However, some corroborative evidence to confirm the connection with Faccombe would be valuable. There were two possibilities: the existence of a Bishop's transcript of the missing registers, or wills which mentioned the family.

Enquiry of the Diocesan Registrar (the Bishops' Transcripts for Hampshire are now at the Hampshire Record Office) for the transcripts was very disappointing; apart from one or two odd years of one or two odd parishes there was nothing before about 1780.

In the matter of wills I thought it advisable to see all the Willis wills at Winchester from the Civil War to 1800, which I did, making short abstracts (see p.41) of each, but only one seemed as if it might have a connection with the family. The will of John Willis of Faccombe made in December 1679 and proved in 1681 mentioned a son John and grandsons John and Peter; these relationships corresponded with the parish register record, Peter having been baptised in November 1679. The grandson in the will was evidently the John baptised in 1678 and the presumed father of the pipemaker. The will with its inventory is reproduced on plates 5 and 6 and transcribed on pp.31 and 33. The will produced the new information that the testator was a 'yeoman', while the inventory, by its description of the contents, gives an interesting picture of the homestead.

However, this will did no more than confirm what was already known from the parish register. Another possibility was the will of a relative on the maternal side of the family and, since John was married in 1677 to Susannah White, I searched for the surname

White in the indexes to wills at Winchester. I found a will of Walter White of East Woodhay made in 1711 and proved in 1714, which appointed his son-in-law John Willis sole executor, and mentioned his grandson John Willis. Walter White was evidently the father of Susannah who married in 1677.

Another interesting connection in this will is that Walter White mentioned his daughter Ann Harding. In the register of St Maurice, Winchester, among other entries for our family, is recorded the burial of Ann Harding Willis in 1779. Did Ann Harding perhaps die a childless widow and leave money to the Willis family who named a daughter after her?

There was a further White will recorded for East Woodhay, that of another Walter White, dated 1728 and proved in 1731; unfortunately it throws no further light on the Willis family connection.

A new clue appeared quite by chance when a genealogist friend was searching the records of the Weavers' Company of London and happened to come across an apprenticeship of a John Willis to a Walter White, dated 21 July 1712. There was no mention of the locality from which they had come, and both White and Willis are not uncommon names, but the coincidence to the two, and the Christian name Walter, was interesting, especially in view of the date. I had always been puzzled by the date of the pipemaker's apprenticeship (1715), when he would have been about 15-16 years old, whereas apprenticeship usually began at 13-14.

If Walter White junior (whose will was proved in 1731) was a weaver in London, several things would be explained. It would be natural for him to take his nephew John as an apprentice, and the idea of a relationship is supported by the fact that this apprenticeship does not appear in the Inland Revenue records (see p.57), indicating that no premium was paid. Moreover, it would be more natural for Walter White senior to have made his son-in-law, who was on the spot, his executor, rather than his absent son. When this Walter died, in 1714, his son, the weaver, may have left

London and returned to East Woodhay, bringing young John Willis with him and apprenticing him locally to a pipemaker.

From the above it will be seen how circumstantial evidence can be pieced together to make a reasonable case. It seems very likely that John Willis (baptised 1678) was married about 1698 and that his son John, born soon after, was the pipemaker, apprenticed in 1715, married in 1718, and father of John who was married in Winchester in 1743.

Assuming this to be the case, the Faccombe family, as appearing from the registers, could be added to the family tree. True, the marriage of John who was baptised in 1622 and buried in 1681 was not recorded, but this would have been during the time of the Civil War, when there was a gap in the Faccombe marriage registers from 1646-1662 (his first child was baptised in 1650).

There is one other loose thread in the pedigree of the Faccombe family: there is no record of the baptism of the first John, son of Richard. It would be quite possible for him to have been baptised in his mother's parish or even, if Richard was the first Willis in Faccombe, in the parish from which his father came. There is no knowing where this may have been, but it may be found one day.

As happens so often in genealogy, there are some weak links in the chain, and a court of law might well throw out my case with the Scottish verdict of 'not proven', but the probability is very strong and only a few extra pieces of evidence would be required to complete the jigsaw puzzle.

While searching for this evidence I was at the same time on the look-out to see what detail I could fill in of the lives of those whose names I recorded. What follows will give some account of my discoveries.

# Filling in the Detail

I started with the county archives in Winchester, which included a good library of topographical and historical works on Hampshire and other books relating to the county. First of all, the name Willis was looked up in a card index, but nothing of relevance was found.

Several early poll books were in the library, the earliest dated 1713, which mentions the family of John of the Soke. The 1779 and 1790 poll books made no mention of Willis in Winchester, but that for 1806 includes John Willis.

I also enquired about rolls of freemen of the City to see whether I could identify the John Willis who became a freeman in 1730, but the Public Library had none that went back as far as that. They did, however, have a record of James Willis being admitted a freeman on 9 October 1828. Eventually I ascertained that the freeman of 1730 was the son of Richard Willis, Bishop of Winchester, but so far as is known he was no relation.

I went on to inspect a variety of documents in the Muniment Room at the Library, which included a large collection of City leases, then only partly indexed. On turning these over, I came across one or two relating to the family. One was a lease dated in 1789 to John Willis, victualler, of vacant ground 'whereon the Church of St George sometime did stand'.

This John was later identified as the John who died in 1820, and on reference to old maps I discovered the location of St George's Church and was able to visit the site, where I found a building which evidently dated from about 1800.

Another lease was dated 1815, granting premises in the High Street to John Willis of the City of Salisbury, and further leases of

1829 and 1843 granted the same property to James Willis, painter. Why was John described as of Salisbury? It is known that he was of Winchester when his daughter Ann married in 1809, but her husband was a Salisbury man, so possibly John had retired and gone to live with or near his daughter. He may have taken the lease for his son James.

James's name occurred in 1850 when, with a grocer, Edward Marmon, he took a lease of the Fish, Poultry and Butchers' markets for a year, with the tolls for weighing cheese, etc., at the three annual fairs, for which they paid £91. Presumably they let out the sites of the stalls at a profit.

Further references to the Willis family were found in a Muster Roll of the 'Winchester Volunteers' for 1806, a Land Tax list for 1796-7, and directories for Hampshire from the 1780s to the 1860s.

Local newspapers provided information of a more sensational nature, such as this, from *The Hampshire Chronicle*:

6 March 1837 'Last evening a man in the employ of Mr. Willis, painter, was returning home with a load of turf with a horse and cart, the animal took fright when the man fell under the wheel and fractured his leg so severely as to render immediate amputation necessary.'

No Workmen's Compensation Act, still less a National Insurance Act! I hope James was generous.

A good deal of time could yet be spent in the Library Muniment Room or with the files of *The Hampshire Chronicle*, but it will be seen from the above that quite a lot of information has been gathered about the life of the family in Winchester.

Another source of information suggested itself following the discovery of the settlement certificates among the parish records of St Maurice, Winchester. I hoped there might be records of the interrogation leading up to the settlement certificate, but the 'Book of Examinations' found there did not begin until 1781.

There was, however, a collection of old rate books, in which the name Willis first appears in March and September 1757, when 'Widow Willis' was listed. In 1759 the name does not appear, so it looks as though the burial at St Maurice of Mary Willis in 1758 was this widow Willis, no doubt Mary (née Marchant), mother of John who was married in 1743.

The name appears again thus:

| 1770 | 19 Apl | Middle Brooks | Mr. Willis |
| 1772 | 19 Mar | Middle Brooks | John Willis |

The name of John Willis continues until 1783 when the entries are:

| 4th Aug. | Middle Brooks | Mr. Willis |
| 19th Sept. | Middle Brooks | Mrs. Willice [sic]. |

John was buried on 3 August 1783, and evidently his widow continued in occupation.

From 1785 there are two entries in each date, both Mr. Willis and Mrs. Willis being mentioned, being John the younger and his mother. The name continues until 1805, when it disappears by May of that year; this, no doubt, is when the family moved to St Thomas's parish.

Turning to other ecclesiastical records, I thought it might be worthwhile seeing the original record of the marriage allegation of John the pipemaker in 1718. This was produced for me (see plate 7, p.44) and, besides giving John's signature, it provided the new information that the bondsman was a Roger Pond, also of Hursley and a pipemaker; this seemed to show that John did indeed work in Hursley.

With the other documents at the Diocesan Registry I found a series of Visitation Books, recording the names of clergy and churchwardens in each parish. Under dates 1686 and 1687 John Willis appears as churchwarden at Faccombe, as did an earlier John in 1641 and 1642. Henry John Willis was churchwarden of St Thomas, Winchester, in 1851 and 1852.

There was a tradition that James Willis of Winchester had been responsible for painting the bosses of the cathedral choir ceiling, many with armorial bearings. I had noticed in the press when these were recently repainted that they had not been done for about a hundred years, so I made enquiry at the Cathedral Library and found there a Treasurer's Book for 1846-60. This showed, among expenses for repairs, payment to Willis in 1851-54, the last including an item of £71 17s. 2d., a substantial sum, evidently for this painting.

While in Winchester, I again searched the indexes to wills, for families who had married into the Willises, bearing in mind the useful information gleaned from the White will, and hoping that other 'in-law' wills might be as helpful. For instance, would any relative of Alice Hellier who married Richard Willis in 1592 mention the family? Such a will might confirm that John who married in 1616 was Richard's son, the baptism not yet being found. The list of Helliers was very long but there were none of Faccombe or Ashmansworth. Wills for Helliers of Hurstbourne Tarrant and Andover were seen, but there was no mention of Willis.

Then there was Rose Sherman who married in 1616, but the name of Sherman again drew a blank. Other names like Marchant, Harding and Jestis were tried also without result.

Following this disappointment I turned to the vast amount of material in the many repositories in London, considering whether there was anything likely to be of help regarding an unimportant provincial family.

Two Johns of Winchester being described as 'painter-stainers', it was worth investigating the records of this City company at the Guildhall Library. I examined the rolls of members and apprentices, but found no mention of the family. The earlier John having been a pipemaker, I looked for the records of the Tobacco-pipe Makers' Company, but there appeared to be no records extant, except a copy of their charter.

At the Public Record Office information might be available if the family had been concerned in law cases. The examination of the index to Chancery Proceedings and Feet of Fines is a long business, but may be worth working through as occasion arises, perhaps while awaiting the arrival of other documents that have been ordered.

I also enquired at the P.R.O. about manorial records. Quite possibly a 'yeoman', or substantial farmer, would be a tenant of the local manor. I asked about the manors of Faccombe, East Woodhay and Ashmansworth, and was advised that there were manorial rolls of Faccombe in the British Museum, and that there were at the P.R.O., among the records of the Ecclesiastical Commission, documents of the manors of East Woodhay and Ashmansworth (now deposited at the County Record Office in Winchester).

I found the Faccombe manor rolls, but unfortunately they were a very irregular series with many gaps. The roll of a Court held on 20 October 1653 (Add. Charters 5077) is illustrated in plate 9 (p.74) and it will be seen that John Willis the elder is among those sworn. At the foot (beginning with the line projecting into the margin) will be seen:

> The note of the tenants' houses that are out of repayre followeth
> ...
>
> ...
> Jo: Willis th'onger (widow Goodfellow's tenant): the dwelling houses wants thatching the barne at the end groundpining.

In two earlier rolls, of October 1592 and March 1592/3 (Add. Charters 5070, 5072), Richard Wyllys presents his excuses through Thomas Hellyar. This is interesting as showing that Richard who married at Faccombe in 1592 was already of sufficient standing as a tenant of the manor to be one of the sworn jurors, and of course Hellyar (or Hellier) was the name of his bride, so it looks as though she may have been of the same village.

I examined the list of manorial records which included those for East Woodhay and Ashmansworth, and found them to be very extensive. I examined one or two volumes of likely date, consisting of presentments, fines, etc. This is still in progress and, as a spare-time occupation, will take some time.

A puzzle of fairly modern times still worried me: Henry John Willis's marriage had not been found in Winchester and he seems to have left no will. I had the 1851 Census Returns for Winchester searched, and found the entry for his household (see plate 2, p.11). He was still a painter, and his three children are entered as 'scholars' and their places of birth given. The eldest was born in Pimlico.

It seemed that this might be a clue to Henry's place of marriage, so searches were made in the Westminster parishes of St Peter Eaton Square and St John Smith Square, but without success. Turning to marriage licences, I found the entry I was seeking among the Faculty Office licences. The particulars showed that the marriage took place at St James Westminster, and a copy of the marriage certificate was obtained from the vicar. If it were not for the clue given by the census return, there would have been no reason to think that marriage was in London.

# Where Next?

It seems clear that the right to armorial bearings, the examination of which was one of the reasons for my quest, is a myth. The arms were probably assumed by James of Winchester, the flame of aldermanic pride being, perhaps, fanned by heraldic study undertaken in the course of trade. The Hampshire branch of the armigerous family have, in any case, been by-passed.

As to the pedigree, having come to a full-stop with the marriage in 1592 at Faccombe, I looked around to see what prospect there was of finding anything earlier. I examined the calendar of early wills (before 1660) at Winchester and found two families at Ecchinswell, which is not far from Faccombe. Both wills were proved in 1570; one, of Nicholas Willes, mentions sons John and William, the other, of Richard Wyllis, mentions a son John. Both spellings are variants of the same name, so the two Johns in the same village make rather a complication. Neither will mentions any Richard who might be the one married at Faccombe in 1592. The latter will might be that of his grandfather, John being perhaps the father (whose name was carried on), but there is no evidence in the wills.

In view of the proximity of this family it was worth searching the registers of Kingsclere (which included Ecchinswell at that date). The result of this search was disappointing. There is a John Willis married in 1575, but this would be too late for a father of Richard, who was apparently established in Faccombe when he married there in 1592. There is a baptism of a Richard Welles in 1567 which might be the Faccombe man but, as it is clear from other entries that there was a separate family named Welles, this is unlikely.

The Kingsclere register was also examined for the baptism of John, son of Richard of Faccombe, which, if there, might indicate that the move had been from Kingsclere. However, there was no trace, although unfortunately some 30 lines in the baptism registers between 1594 and 1597 are illegible.

Looking at the records of registers in surrounding villages, I found that early registers were still extant for Hurstbourne Tarrant, and tried on the chance for the baptism of John in 1593-8, but without success. Richard might have come from some distant place and an unexpected clue might some day appear.

The manorial records of Ecchinswell might produce some information. They are very extensive and it would take some time to go through them. The Willis wills at Winchester seem to be exhausted, though one day a will of another name may turn out to mention the family and provide a clue. In short, it looks rather as if, while keeping a look-out for possibilities, I must, like Mr. Micawber, wait for 'something to turn up'.

# THE FAMILY OF
# WILLIS

## OF FACCOMBE AND WINCHESTER, HANTS., AND EALING, MIDDLESEX

Notes:

Richard Wyllys appears in the Court Roll of Faccombe Manor, 22 October 1592, and 22 March 1592/3 as excused from service as juror (B.M. Add. Ch.5070, 5072)

Burials at Faccombe: Alice Willis, 29 July 1646. Alice Willis, 23 July 1673 (2 burials for 3 Alices–? which).

John Willis m. Margerie Waterman at Linkenholt, 9 October 1637. ? second marriage of John m. Rose Sherman. No issue found at Linkenholt.

A Luke Willis was buried at St Maurice, Winchester, 2 January 1780. He may have been son of Luke of Ashmansworth (buried 1757) at Faccombe.

The burial of John Willis in 1742, assumed to be that of John (born 1678), might be that of John the pipe-maker (married 1718). There is a burial of a John Willis at Hamstead Marshall 18 December 1715, which might be that of John (born 1678).

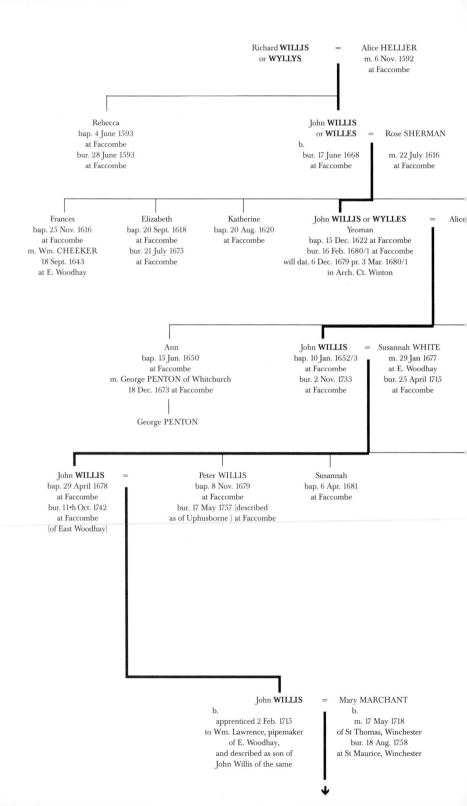

Richard **WILLIS**  =  Alice HELLIER
or **WYLLYS**        m. 6 Nov. 1592
                     at Faccombe

Rebecca                          John **WILLIS**  =  Rose SHERMAN
bap. 4 June 1593                 or **WILLES**
at Faccombe                      b.
bur. 28 June 1593                bur. 17 June 1668     m. 22 July 1616
at Faccombe                      at Faccombe           at Faccombe

Frances                Elizabeth                Katherine              John **WILLIS** or **WYLLES**  =  Alice
bap. 25 Nov. 1616      bap. 20 Sept. 1618       bap. 20 Aug. 1620      Yeoman
at Faccombe            at Faccombe              at Faccombe            bap. 15 Dec. 1622 at Faccombe
m. Wm. CHEEKER        bur. 21 July 1675                                bur. 16 Feb. 1680/1 at Faccombe
18 Sept. 1643          at Faccombe                                     will dat. 6 Dec. 1679 pr. 3 Mar. 1680/1
at E. Woodhay                                                          in Arch. Ct. Winton

                       Ann                              John **WILLIS**  =  Susannah WHITE
                       bap. 15 Jun. 1650                bap. 10 Jan. 1652/3   m. 29 Jan 1677
                       at Faccombe                      at Faccombe           at E. Woodhay
                       m. George PENTON of Whitchurch   bur. 2 Nov. 1733      bur. 25 April 1715
                       18 Dec. 1673 at Faccombe         at Faccombe           at Faccombe

                       George PENTON

John **WILLIS**          =        Peter WILLIS                    Susannah
bap. 29 April 1678               bap. 8 Nov. 1679                 bap. 6 Apr. 1681
at Faccombe                      at Faccombe                      at Faccombe
bur. 11•h Oct. 1742              bur. 17 May 1757 (described
at Faccombe                      as of Uphusborne ) at Faccombe
(of East Woodhay)

                                 John **WILLIS**          =  Mary MARCHANT
                                 b.                          b.
                                 apprenticed 2 Feb. 1715     m. 17 May 1718
                                 to Wm. Lawrence, pipemaker   of St Thomas, Winchester
                                 of E. Woodhay,              bur. 18 Aug. 1758
                                 and described as son of     at St Maurice, Winchester
                                 John Willis of the same

                                 ↓

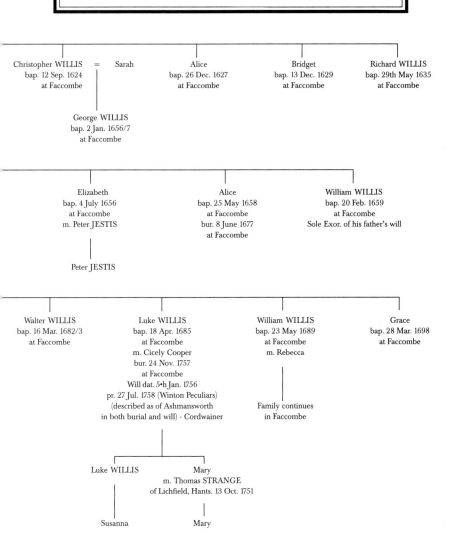

# THE FAMILY OF
# WILLIS
## OF FACCOMBE AND WINCHESTER, HANTS.,
## AND EALING, MIDDLESEX

Christopher WILLIS   =   Sarah
bap. 12 Sep. 1624
at Faccombe

Alice
bap. 26 Dec. 1627
at Faccombe

Bridget
bap. 13 Dec. 1629
at Faccombe

Richard WILLIS
bap. 29th May 1635
at Faccombe

George WILLIS
bap. 2 Jan. 1656/7
at Faccombe

Elizabeth
bap. 4 July 1656
at Faccombe
m. Peter JESTIS

Alice
bap. 25 May 1658
at Faccombe
bur. 8 June 1677
at Faccombe

William WILLIS
bap. 20 Feb. 1659
at Faccombe
Sole Exor. of his father's will

Peter JESTIS

Walter WILLIS
bap. 16 Mar. 1682/3
at Faccombe

Luke WILLIS
bap. 18 Apr. 1685
at Faccombe
m. Cicely Cooper
bur. 24 Nov. 1757
at Faccombe
Will dat. 5•h Jan. 1756
pr. 27 Jul. 1758 (Winton Peculiars)
(described as of Ashmansworth
in both burial and will) - Cordwainer

William WILLIS
bap. 23 May 1689
at Faccombe
m. Rebecca

Grace
bap. 28 Mar. 1698
at Faccombe

Family continues
in Faccombe

Luke WILLIS

Mary
m. Thomas STRANGE
of Lichfield, Hants. 13 Oct. 1751

Susanna

Mary

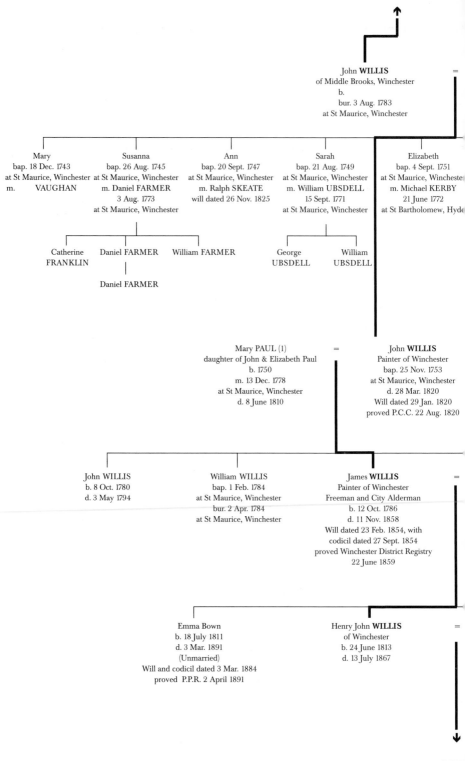

John **WILLIS**
of Middle Brooks, Winchester
b.
bur. 3 Aug. 1783
at St Maurice, Winchester
=

| Mary | Susanna | Ann | Sarah | Elizabeth |
|---|---|---|---|---|
| bap. 18 Dec. 1743 | bap. 26 Aug. 1745 | bap. 20 Sept. 1747 | bap. 21 Aug. 1749 | bap. 4 Sept. 1751 |
| at St Maurice, Winchester | at St Maurice, Winchester | at St Maurice, Winchester | at St Maurice, Winchester | at St Maurice, Wincheste |
| m.    VAUGHAN | m. Daniel FARMER | m. Ralph SKEATE | m. William UBSDELL | m. Michael KERBY |
|  | 3 Aug. 1773 | will dated 26 Nov. 1825 | 15 Sept. 1771 | 21 June 1772 |
|  | at St Maurice, Winchester |  | at St Maurice, Winchester | at St Bartholomew, Hyde |

Catherine        Daniel FARMER      William FARMER
FRANKLIN
                    |
           Daniel FARMER

George        William
UBSDELL      UBSDELL

Mary PAUL (1)                                    =        John **WILLIS**
daughter of John & Elizabeth Paul                        Painter of Winchester
b. 1750                                                   bap. 25 Nov. 1753
m. 13 Dec. 1778                                          at St Maurice, Winchester
at St Maurice, Winchester                                d. 28 Mar. 1820
d. 8 June 1810                                           Will dated 29 Jan. 1820
                                                         proved P.C.C. 22 Aug. 1820

| John WILLIS | William WILLIS | James **WILLIS** |
|---|---|---|
| b. 8 Oct. 1780 | bap. 1 Feb. 1784 | Painter of Winchester |
| d. 3 May 1794 | at St Maurice, Winchester | Freeman and City Alderman |
|  | bur. 2 Apr. 1784 | b. 12 Oct. 1786 |
|  | at St Maurice, Winchester | d. 11 Nov. 1858 |
|  |  | Will dated 23 Feb. 1854, with |
|  |  | codicil dated 27 Sept. 1854 |
|  |  | proved Winchester District Registry |
|  |  | 22 June 1859 |

=

Emma Bown                                    Henry John **WILLIS**
b. 18 July 1811                              of Winchester
d. 3 Mar. 1891                               b. 24 June 1813
(Unmarried)                                  d. 13 July 1867
Will and codicil dated 3 Mar. 1884
proved  P.P.R. 2 April 1891

=

James WILL

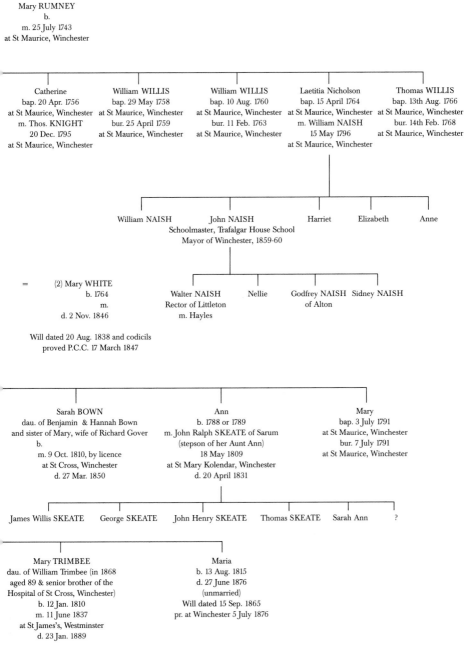

Mary RUMNEY
b.
m. 25 July 1743
at St Maurice, Winchester

Catherine
bap. 20 Apr. 1756
at St Maurice, Winchester
m. Thos. KNIGHT
20 Dec. 1795
at St Maurice, Winchester

William WILLIS
bap. 29 May 1758
at St Maurice, Winchester
bur. 25 April 1759
at St Maurice, Winchester

William WILLIS
bap. 10 Aug. 1760
at St Maurice, Winchester
bur. 11 Feb. 1763
at St Maurice, Winchester

Laetitia Nicholson
bap. 15 April 1764
at St Maurice, Winchester
m. William NAISH
15 May 1796
at St Maurice, Winchester

Thomas WILLIS
bap. 13th Aug. 1766
at St Maurice, Winchester
bur. 14th Feb. 1768
at St Maurice, Winchester

William NAISH

John NAISH
Schoolmaster, Trafalgar House School
Mayor of Winchester, 1859-60

Harriet

Elizabeth

Anne

=    (2) Mary WHITE
b. 1764
m.
d. 2 Nov. 1846

Will dated 20 Aug. 1838 and codicils
proved P.C.C. 17 March 1847

Walter NAISH
Rector of Littleton
m. Hayles

Nellie

Godfrey NAISH
of Alton

Sidney NAISH

Sarah BOWN
dau. of Benjamin & Hannah Bown
and sister of Mary, wife of Richard Gover
b.
m. 9 Oct. 1810, by licence
at St Cross, Winchester
d. 27 Mar. 1850

Ann
b. 1788 or 1789
m. John Ralph SKEATE of Sarum
(stepson of her Aunt Ann)
18 May 1809
at St Mary Kolendar, Winchester
d. 20 April 1831

Mary
bap. 3 July 1791
at St Maurice, Winchester
bur. 7 July 1791
at St Maurice, Winchester

James Willis SKEATE    George SKEATE    John Henry SKEATE    Thomas SKEATE    Sarah Ann    ?

Mary TRIMBEE
dau. of William Trimbee (in 1868
aged 89 & senior brother of the
Hospital of St Cross, Winchester)
b. 12 Jan. 1810
m. 11 June 1837
at St James's, Westminster
d. 23 Jan. 1889

Maria
b. 13 Aug. 1815
d. 27 June 1876
(unmarried)
Will dated 15 Sep. 1865
pr. at Winchester 5 July 1876

Sarah Elizabeth
b. 28 June 1837
m. Richard SNOW
Miller, of Abbotsworthy, Winchester
25 Jan. 1865
at St Peter, Cheesehill, Winchester

↓

James Herbert **WILLIS** L.R.I.B.A. = Annie Elizabeth PAPAZOGLU
Architect, H.M. Office of Works dau. of George & Sarah Papazoglu
of Ealing, Middlesex and the b. 13 Aug. 1871
British Embassy, Constantinople m. 29 Jan. 1894
b. 4 March 1864 at British Consulate General and
d. 15 Dec. 1950 Constantinople
Will dated 17 Nov. 1944 and d. 24 Mar. 1939
codicil dated 14 Mar. 1947
proved P.P.R. 24 Jan. 1951

Arthur James **WILLIS** F.R.I.C.S. = Audrey Isabel Edith Thompson
Chartered Quantity Surveyor dau. of Thomas Moore-Lane and
of Ealing, Middlesex and Isabel Mary THOMPSON of Ealing
Lyminge, Kent b. 5 July 1897
b. 16 Jan. 1895 m. at St John's, Ealing
at Constantinople 3 Aug. 1918
d. 26 Nov. 1983 d. 29 Sept. 1981

Cicely Mary = John Norman CAPENER Christopher James **WILLIS** F.R.I.C.S.
B.A. (Lond.) M.A. (Cantab.), M.I.C.E. b. 25 May 1928
b. 29 Nov. 1922 son of Norman Capener, F.R.C.S. at Ealing, Middlesex
m. Lyminge, Kent of Exeter, Devon
17 June 1950 b. 23 Aug. 1924

↓

James Andrew **WILLIS** = Moira Patricia Jane Rosemary
B.Sc., F.R.I.C.S., dau. of Dermot b. 28 Jan. 1959
Dip.Arb., A.C.I.Arb James and d. 28 Jan. 1960
Chartered Quantity Surveyor Eileen RUSSELL
of New Malden, Surrey b. 28 May 1957
b. 2 Oct. 1957 m. 15 Oct. 1983

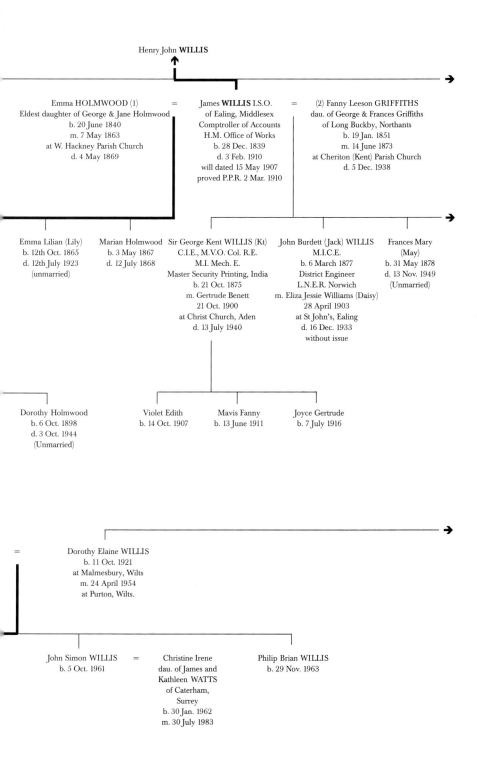

Henry John **WILLIS**

Emma HOLMWOOD (1)
Eldest daughter of George & Jane Holmwood
b. 20 June 1840
m. 7 May 1863
at W. Hackney Parish Church
d. 4 May 1869

=

James **WILLIS** I.S.O.
of Ealing, Middlesex
Comptroller of Accounts
H.M. Office of Works
b. 28 Dec. 1839
d. 3 Feb. 1910
will dated 15 May 1907
proved P.P.R. 2 Mar. 1910

=

(2) Fanny Leeson GRIFFITHS
dau. of George & Frances Griffiths
of Long Buckby, Northants
b. 19 Jan. 1851
m. 14 June 1873
at Cheriton (Kent) Parish Church
d. 5 Dec. 1938

Emma Lilian (Lily)
b. 12th Oct. 1865
d. 12th July 1923
(unmarried)

Marian Holmwood
b. 3 May 1867
d. 12 July 1868

Sir George Kent WILLIS (Kt)
C.I.E., M.V.O. Col. R.E.
M.I. Mech. E.
Master Security Printing, India
b. 21 Oct. 1875
m. Gertrude Benett
21 Oct. 1900
at Christ Church, Aden
d. 13 July 1940

John Burdett (Jack) WILLIS
M.I.C.E.
b. 6 March 1877
District Engineer
L.N.E.R. Norwich
m. Eliza Jessie Williams (Daisy)
28 April 1903
at St John's, Ealing
d. 16 Dec. 1933
without issue

Frances Mary
(May)
b. 31 May 1878
d. 13 Nov. 1949
(Unmarried)

Dorothy Holmwood
b. 6 Oct. 1898
d. 3 Oct. 1944
(Unmarried)

Violet Edith
b. 14 Oct. 1907

Mavis Fanny
b. 13 June 1911

Joyce Gertrude
b. 7 July 1916

=

Dorothy Elaine WILLIS
b. 11 Oct. 1921
at Malmesbury, Wilts
m. 24 April 1954
at Purton, Wilts.

John Simon WILLIS
b. 5 Oct. 1961

=

Christine Irene
dau. of James and
Kathleen WATTS
of Caterham,
Surrey
b. 30 Jan. 1962
m. 30 July 1983

Philip Brian WILLIS
b. 29 Nov. 1963

←——————————————————————————————————┐

Emma
b. 5 Nov. 1841
m. Thomas Alfred JONES
Jeweller, of Islington
at St Paul's Islington
5 May 1863

↓

←——————————————┬————————————————————┬————————————————————┐

Frank Reginald WILLIS
C.B.E., Capt. R.N.
Chief Inspector of Naval
Ordnance, Admiralty
b. 9 Aug. 1881
m. Pauline Mann (Poppy)
14 May 1908
at St John's, Ealing
d. 8 April 1964

Richard WILLIS
M.A. (Oxon.)
b. 24 June 1887
Temp. Lieut. Loyal N. Lancs.
Regt. killed in Action
16 May 1916
(Unmarried)

Norman Steward WILLIS
M.A. (Oxon.) Vicar of
Purton, Wilts. & Hon.
Canon of Bristol
b. 29 Oct. 1894
m. Eileen Mary Burke
at St John's, Ealing
1 March 1919

Frances Mary (Molly)
B.Sc. (Lond.)
b. 24 Mar. 1909
d. 2 July 1980
(unmarried)

Eugenie Leeson
M.A., M.B., B.Ch. (Cantab.)
F.R.C.S., L.R.C.P.
b. 23 July 1910
d. 12 Sept. 1948
(unmarried)

Pamela Leslie
B.A. (Cantab.)
b. 28 Mar. 1914

Angela Christine
M.B., B.Ch.
b. 23 June 1929
m. Denis FOWLER
M.B., B.Ch.

←——————————————————————————————————┘

# Index

Note: page numbers in bold type refer to Plates

References are included to the aspects of *A Genealogical Adventure* most likely to be helpful to readers of this book.

NOTES